Mark Twain's

A CONNECTICUT YANKEE IN KING ARTHUR'S COURT

AND

THE MYSTERIOUS STRANGER

LIFE ON THE MISSISSIPPI

CHARLES LEAVITT
ASSISTANT PROFESSOR OF ENGLISH
MONTCLAIR STATE COLLEGE

MONARCH PRESS

Published by
MONARCH PRESS
a Simon & Schuster division of
Gulf & Western Corporation
Simon & Schuster Building
1230 Avenue of the Americas
New York, N.Y. 10020

Standard Book Number: 0-671-00879-X

Library of Congress Card Number: 66-27337

Printed in the United States of America

CONTENTS

one *THE AUTHOR: MARK TWAIN* **5**

The life of Mark Twain; his work, and influences on his writing *5*

A chronological list of the works of Mark Twain *14*

two *A CONNECTICUT YANKEE IN KING ARTHUR'S COURT* **16**

Brief summary of the plot *16*

Detailed summary with analytic comment *19*

Description and analysis of the characters *52*

three *THE MYSTERIOUS STRANGER* **56**

Brief summary of the plot *56*

Detailed summary with analytic comment *58*

Description and analysis of the characters *68*

four *LIFE ON THE MISSISSIPPI* **70**

Brief summary *70*

Detailed summary with analytic comment *72*

five *COMMENTARY* **81**

An historical survey of criticism on the works of Mark Twain

six *TEST QUESTIONS* **87**

Essay questions and detailed answers

seven *FURTHER READING* **95**

A bibliography for the author and his work, and a guide to further reading

BRIEF SUMMARY OF MARK TWAIN'S LIFE AND WORKS

HANNIBAL AND THE MISSISSIPPI RIVER: Mark Twain (the pen name for Samuel Langhorne Clemens) was born November 30, 1835, in the tiny village of Florida, Missouri. Both of his parents were descendants of Virginians. His mother's people claimed connections with Southern aristocracy; his father, a dreamer with little talent for earning much money, was at various times a storekeeper and lawyer. When Samuel Clemens was four years old, his family moved to Hannibal, Missouri, a town on the Mississippi River. Hannibal, a town almost geographically in the center of the United States, was alive with endless streams of people and continuous activities which stimulated the imagination of the boy who was to become Mark Twain. Of particular fascination to young Twain was the constant arrivals of steamboats. He was as anxious to become a river pilot as an early-twentieth-century lad was eager to become a railroad engineer—or a mid-twentieth century boy would anticipate becoming a jet pilot or an astronaut.

After attending school until when Twain was about twelve years old, his father died. The next year Mark Twain was apprenticed to a printer. By 1851, he was working for his brother, Orion, who had become a newspaper publisher in Hannibal. Like Ben Franklin, Twain's first approach to literature was through typesetting for a newspaper. Among the items Twain set in type were humorous articles and sketches. He, himself, contributed a few attempts at humor to his brother's newspaper, the *Journal*. Finally, he left Orion's employment, and he joined the staffs of one newspaper after another, ranging from St. Louis, New York City and Philadelphia to Keokuk, Iowa, where he rejoined his printer brother to continue his trade as a typesetter. In 1856, in his twenty-first year, he concluded his career in a printer's shop. He wrote some comic travel letters for the *Keokuk Saturday Post.* The letters were signed with the pseudonym Thomas Jefferson Snodgrass, and they were typical of the humorous attempts of the period. They purposely had misspellings, very bad grammar and strangely constructed sentences.

Finally, Twain embarked on a boat traveling down the Mississippi River. His object was South America, where he hoped to make a quick fortune in Brazil. Finding difficulty in booking passage to his destination, he tried a different route to fortune and became an apprentice to Horace Bixby, a superior river pilot. His intensive training lasted for a year and a half, during which time he learned the Mississippi River thoroughly—up and down, by night and by day. For about four years, Twain worked as a river pilot and enjoyed the work which provided constant excitment. He became keenly aware of the importance of observing details. Many of the detailed descriptions of nature in his writings were probably the result of his intense observation of Mississippi River life during his days as a river pilot.

THE WEST, EARLY PUBLICATIONS, AND THE LECTURE CIRCUIT: By the spring of 1861, the Civil War had stopped river traffic to a considerable degree. For a few weeks, Twain was an unhappy participator on the Confederate side. He later described his reaction in the sketch, "The Campaign That Failed." Disgusted with the ineffectiveness of war-making in Missouri, Twain joined his brother Orion who was journeying to the Nevada territory to become Territorial Secretary. During the late summer of 1861, Twain found himself in Carson City, Nevada territory, where he worked unsuccessfully with a timber operation and a mining speculation. In 1862, he accepted a post as feature editor for a Nevada newspaper, the *Virginia City Territorial Enterprise.* As he traveled through the Nevada territory, noting how people lived in frontier mining towns, he gained experiences which later became incorporated into his novels. Sometimes, in Mark Twain's stories of England of long ago, such as *A Connecticut Yankee in King Arthur's Court* or *The Prince and the Pauper,* one senses that a character description is based directly on some memorable person observed by feature editor Twain in the Nevada territory. When he was covering the Nevada constitutional convention, Samuel Langhorne Clemens officially adopted for himself the pen name

"Mark Twain" (a phrase meaning "two fathoms deep" when a member of a riverboat crew takes a sounding for the depth of the water near a boat).

By 1864, Twain was in San Francisco, writing for newspapers and periodicals. Fascinated with a tall tale he heard, he wrote it up as "The Celebrated Jumping Frog of Calaveras County." Published in the New York *Saturday Press* for November 18, 1865, it won him almost instant recognition throughout America. In 1866, he went to the Sandwich Islands in the Pacific Ocean, and wrote travel reports. About this time, he began the first of the many series of lectures he delivered.

EUROPE, MARRIAGE, AND AUTOBIOGRAPHICAL TRAVEL WORKS: Late in 1866, Mark Twain began a tour as a traveling correspondent for a newspaper, the *San Francisco Alta California.* He wrote travel letters about American cities, such as New York and St. Louis. After lecturing successfully in Eastern and Midwestern cities, he began, on June 8, 1867, an excursion to Europe and the Near East. The letters sent back to America were eventually published as *Innocents Abroad* (1869). Twain not only satirizes the ancestor-worship of visiting Americans, but he also pokes fun at the typical tourist who cannot see beyond his guide book. *Innocents Abroad* sold many copies. In 1867, Twain met Olivia Langdon, a charming young woman from Elmira, New York. Her health was never too good, and toward the end of her life, she became a semi-invalid. They were married in 1870. At first they lived in Buffalo, New York; later they moved to Hartford, Connecticut, where they lived until 1891. Here Twain wrote a book of his experiences in the West, published in 1872 as *Roughing It.* In 1875, a number of chapters concerning his apprentice and piloting days on the Mississippi River were published serially in the *Atlantic Monthly* under the title, "Old Times on the Mississippi." Later Twain revisited the river of his youth and wrote more about the Mississippi–from an adult tourist point of view. The exciting "Old Times on the Mississippi" was combined with the later and less interesting chapters, and the result was published in 1883 as *Life on The Mississippi.* Other books based upon his travels were *A Tramp Abroad* (1880) and *Following the Equator* (1897).

NOVELS OF POLITICAL SATIRE AND OF YOUTH: Mark Twain's first attempt at writing a novel was in collaboration with a Hartford neighbor Charles Dudley Warner. The work was *The Gilded Age* (1873), a satire against the legislative corruption Twain observed when he lived in Washington, D. C., 1867-1868. (Undoubtedly, the governmental corruption of the 1870's must have offered Twain and Warner a ready topic for their combined talents.) *The Gilded Age* also attacked speculation and "improvements" designed to fill the pockets of political party members. As weak as *The Gilded Age* is as a novel, its re-creation of an historical era makes it worthy of being read. Also, it features one of Twain's finest characterizations, Colonel Sellers–a Mr. Micawber type of "fair weather tomorrow" gentleman; modeled, in part, on Mark Twain's own father, who was eternally optimistic, but usually unsuccessful. Colonel Sellers appears in a later novel, *The American Claimant* (1892). In this rather unsuccessful, but interesting romantic tale, Colonel Sellers is the American descendant of an heir to an English estate and title. Twain's satiric knife is keen when he describes the true English heir's reactions to America. The young man attempts to become noticed in America without money. He is surprised at how much more attention is paid to him when his true identity and resources are made public.

Mark Twain's stories appear to be predominantly of young people–representative of a variety of backgrounds and temperaments, but always *youths.* Twain shifts gears when he goes from the satire of *The Gilded Age* (1873) to the mischievous robustness of childhood pictured in *The Adventures of Tom Sawyer* (1876). Over the years, *Tom Sawyer* has ranked first among Twain's best sellers. Its sale of over two million copies has even outsold the critically popular *Huckleberry Finn.* Several very successful Hollywood films were based upon *Tom Sawyer.* In *Tom Sawyer,* Twain returns to the deepest mine of his background experience, his own home town, Hannibal, Missouri–identified in *Tom Sawyer* as St. Petersburg. In this easygoing, backwater, small town, perched on the edge of the Mississippi River, grows up a mischievous, but goodhearted, "normal" American youth–Tom. The romance of youth is viewed over and over again in this book, as Tom maneuvers his friends into whitewashing a fence, as he plays hookey from school, and as he explores a mysterious cave. Perhaps one of the most important reasons that *Tom Sawyer* has remained Twain's most popular book with young readers is the fact that it represents high-spirited youth in its reaction against parental and community authority. Its young romantic hero, Tom, is *not* an example of "perfect behavior begets perfect results." Its anti-authority quality allows a youthful reader to feel a sort of kinship with Tom and his adventures. Huckleberry Finn appears as a minor character in *Tom Sawyer.* Eighteen years later, in 1894, Twain attempted, without success, to interest his reading public in another tale of Tom Sawyer, entitled *Tom Sawyer, Abroad.* There was little public response to this novel. Again, he tried–this time in 1896 with *Tom Sawyer, Detective.* The reading public paid little attention to the third Tom Sawyer book.

Another Twain novel of youth, which has always interested young people is *The Prince and the Pauper* (1882), a tale of confused identities. Edward, the Prince of Wales and son of Henry VIII changes clothing with Tom Canty from the slums of London. From that point onward, the gorgeously clothed Tom, the pauper, attempts to govern England from the people's point of view. The poorly clothed Prince Edward discovers what life is like for the underprivileged masses of Englishmen. He encounters injustice after injustice and is amazed that no one recognizes his royal person. Twain not only satirizes ancient feudalism and privileges, but also suggests that externals, such as clothing and the trappings of royalty, are what people often judge by.

The Prince and The Pauper features the adventures of two boys; Twain's acknowledged masterpiece, *The Adventures of Huckleberry Finn* (1884), follows the same pattern. The title character, the fourteen-year-old Huck Finn, tells the story in his own words. Although Huck is practically homeless, uneducated, and a good-natured vagabond, he is realistic and skillfully adapts to the world in which he finds himself. The established world of St. Petersburg constrains his natural activities. Village prejudices and superstitions attempt to subdue Huck, a child of nature. His companion, Tom Sawyer (a romantically minded youngster, in contrast to the realistic Huck), continuously involves Huck in imaginative adventures, such as the raid on the "pirates" and "A-rabs." Huck, the realist, and Tom, the romanticist, react in different ways to their environment—but, almost always, the generous-minded Huck bows to the plans of his high-spirited friend, Tom. When Huck leaves St. Petersburg and travels down the Mississippi River with an escaping Negro slave (Jim), Huck takes the lead. In succeeding episodes as they drift down the river toward New Orleans, the pair use their wits adapting themselves to a wide variety of people.

Twain's brilliant novel of Huck and his travels may be considered through a variety of approaches. The tale of boyish adventure is but the first general level of approach. Twain's rich imagery of Mississippi River Valley life allows the reader a remarkable picture of the South of the 1840's. The satirical treatment of various social evils, such as sentimentalism and racism is thought-provoking. For those especially interested in literary technique, the first person singular narration used (the fourteen-year-old Huck) is effective, along with the use of the picaresque (episodic) method of story structure. As a document in early American realism in fiction, *Huckleberry Finn* rates high in its use of colloquial speech and dialect, as well as its accent on the "anti-hero" (such as "Pop"—Huck's father —and the infamous rascals, the "Duke" and the "King"). Ernest Hemingway was often quoted as saying that realistic American fiction begins with the publication of *Huckleberry Finn.*

HISTORICAL FICTION—TWAIN'S "YANKEE" AND JOAN OF ARC: In 1889, Twain published an historical novel, *A Connecticut Yankee in King Arthur's Court.* This work might be approached on at least two levels. On the surface, it seems to be nineteenth-century science-fiction, a late nineteenth-century munitions maker from Hartford, Connecticut finds himself accidentally propelled into the late sixth century of King Arthur's court at Camelot. Using such strokes of good luck as knowing the exact time of an eclipse and native Yankee ingenuity, the Connecticut Yankee—called "the Boss"—attempts to organize King Arthur's feudalistic kingdom into a Utopia of nineteenth-century perfection. Sometimes the humor is rich but far-fetched, for instance, the rescue by knights on bicycles or the small individual billboards advertising sanitary products, worn by knights on their travels. However, the farcical part of the book is of less importance than is Twain's white-hot attack on injustice, intolerance, and the continual and basic ignorance of men as they willfully and piously mistreat their fellow men. Twain even presents the vulgarity seldom mentioned in romantic stories of lords and ladies of ancient days. The thoughtful reader soon realizes that Mark Twain's historical setting is but a thin mask over his real target of attack–nineteenth century awe for materialism (money, position, power–no matter how acquired). *A Connecticut Yankee* has creeping through it the sad overtones of pessimism, so representative of the last great Twain writings, such as *The Mysterious Stranger.* Mark Twain briefly leaves the European scene for a return to the American South with the novel *Pudd'nhead Wilson* (1894). This less popular work features events in the life of two boys (children of the "Master" and the slave) who, soon after their births, were interchanged in their cradles. The eventual proof of their correct identities is established by the efforts of Puddn'head Wilson who, at their births, recorded the fingerprints of each child.

For a time, the cold, dark pessimism in Twain's writings seemed to suggest that he had begun to lose all faith in any possibility that man might rise to noble heights, demonstrated dramatically in *A Connecticut Yankee.* Then, in 1896, seven years after the publication of Yankee, Twain brought forth a romanticized portrait of one of the great heroines of the world–Joan of Arc. All of the biographical information available about Mark Twain has always suggested his intense admiration of and respect for women. His adoration for his beautiful wife, Olivia, and his untiring devotion to his three daughters, Susie, Clara, and Jean, have been well-established facts. One senses the intoxication in Twain's heart as he penned his tribute to one of the world's great heroines. He felt that his most important literary achievement was *Personal Recollections of Joan of Arc.* In his pictures of ladies in King Arthur's court, he had described beauties motivated by self-interest. In Joan of Arc, he found a heroine worthy of his devotion. The heroic qualities which he found lacking in mankind at large were all realized in the Maid of Orleans. Pureness of heart, loftiness of purpose, and unselfishness of intent–all these virtues he found concentrated in Joan. In order to heighten dramatically Joan's superior moral position, Twain painted her enemies in dark colors. In *Huckleberry Finn,* the unpleasant characters, such as "Pop" and the "Duke" and the "King," are somewhat forgiven for the almost comic sides of their failings. The gorgeous stage of the fifteenth century is described as a series of processions in a medieval masque. The story is narrated from the memory of faithful Louis De Conte. Joan, the focusing character, is splendidly realized. Twain once told a friend, that he enjoyed writing this romance more than any of his other works.

SORROWS AND THE PESSIMISTIC LAST WORKS: In 1894, Mark Twain's financial affairs were in a confused state. Partly because of the Panic of 1893, partly because his publishing firm (established because Twain thought his publishers were defrauding him) sank into insolvency, and partly because of heavy speculation in a typesetting machine which proved to be worthless, he went into bankruptcy. But he soon recovered his fortune. Besides realizing profits from his idealized treatment of Joan of Arc, he made a financially successful lecture tour around the world, which he wrote up into a travel book, *Following the Equator* (1897). His greatest misfortunes at this time were the illnesses and deaths of various loved ones. One of his beloved daughters died, his brother Orion and a sister died, both his wife Olivia and his daughter Jean became invalids and finally Mrs. Clemens died. Twain–America's favorite humorist–turned into a pessimistic writer, whose last works are filled with darkness and grimness. In a long essay, entitled "What Is Man?" (written in 1898 and published in 1906), he expressed his strong belief in determinism–that one's life is unavoidably influenced by the forces of heredity and environment. He argued that men are helpless pawns and that they are motivated in all their actions by selfishness. In the short story, "The Man That Corrupted Hadleyburg," (1899), he illustrated that greed is at the base of most human action. About 1898, he wrote a powerful, strange novelette, *The Mysterious Stranger* (published, after his death, in 1916). In this tale, set in late medieval Austria, Philip Traum ("Satan"), the nephew of the Devil, visits village boys who resemble Huck Finn and Tom Sawyer. He constantly reveals the meanness and selfishness in man to them. "Satan" consoles his unhappy, youthful friends with the thought that, not only he, but all of life may be a dream. He concludes with the thought that perhaps the dreamer of *this* unhappy nightmare may sometime dream "other dreams, and better."

It is somewhat disenchanting to learn that Mark Twain (sometimes called "The Lincoln of our Literature") could travel the long path of success toward a firm place in the hearts of most American readers, only to become, himself, an unhappy frustrated, disappointed old man. How fortunate we are to be able to go back to the inspired and spirited works of his more happy days—to drink at the rich fountains of *Tom Sawyer, Huck Finn, The Prince and the Pauper, A Connecticut Yankee,* and *Life on the Mississippi.*

A CHRONOLOGICAL LIST OF MARK TWAIN'S SEPARATE WORKS

1867	*The Celebrated Jumping Frog of Calaveras County and Other Sketches*
1869	*The Innocents Abroad*
1871	*Mark Twain's (Burlesque) Autobiography*
1872	*Roughing It*
1873	*The Gilded Age (with Charles Dudley Warner)*
1875	*Mark Twain's Sketches: New and Old*
1876	*The Adventures of Tom Sawyer*
1877	*A True Story*
1878	*Punch, Brothers, Punch!*
1880	*A Tramp Abroad*
1882	*The Stolen White Elephant*
1882	*The Prince and The Pauper*
1883	*Life on the Mississippi*
1885	*The Adventures of Huckleberry Finn*
1889	*A Connecticut Yankee in King Arthur's Court*
1892	*The American Claimant*
1892	*Merry Tales*
1893	*The $1,000,000 Bank Note*
1894	*Tom Sawyer Abroad*
1894	*The Tragedy of Pudd'nhead Wilson*
1896	*Personal Recollections of Joan of Arc*
1896	*Tom Sawyer Abroad, Tom Sawyer, Detective, and Other Stories*
1897	*Following the Equator*
1897	*How to Tell a Story and Other Essays*
1900	*The Man That Corrupted Hadleyburg and Other Stories and Essays*
1902	*A Double Barrelled Detective Story*
1903	*My Debut as a Literary Person*
1904	*A Dog's Tale*

1904	*Extracts from Adam's Diary*
1905	*King Leopold's Soliloquy*
1906	*What Is Man?*
1906	*The $30,000 Bequest*
1906	*Eve's Diary*
1907	*Christian Science*
1907	*A Horse's Tale*
1909	*Is Shakespeare Dead?*
1909	*Extract from Captain Stormfield's Visit to Heaven*
1916	*The Mysterious Stranger*
1917	*What Is Man? and Other Essays*
1919	*The Curious Republic of Gondour*
1922	*The Mysterious Stranger and Other Stories*
1923	*Europe and Elsewhere*

BRIEF SUMMARY OF

A CONNECTICUT YANKEE IN KING ARTHUR'S COURT

Hank Morgan, a Connecticut Yankee working in a munitions factory near Hartford, is tapped on the head by a crowbar during a quarrel with a fellow worker. He awakens in the early part of the sixth century, A.D. Captured by the knightly Sir Kay, he is taken to Camelot, King Arthur's court, where the knights of the realm gather around the "Table Round." The Yankee is amazed to hear each knight exaggerate the tale of his own exploits, while searching for the "Holy Grail." The unhappy Hank is sentenced to be burned at the stake on the twenty-first of June. Fortunately, he remembers (from his knowledge of science and history) that there was a total eclipse of the sun on that day. He threatens to blot out the sun if he is harmed. When the eclipse occurs, King Arthur promises the Yankee the second place in the kingdom (next to himself) if the "magician" Hank will bring back the sun. Merlin, previously the leading magician at the court, is jealous at the Yankee's success. He vows revenge for being pushed into the background.

Soon, Hank is familiarly called "the Boss" by everyone. He starts an extensive program of reorganization of King Arthur's kingdom. The Boss can dictate to every group in England (including the knights), except to the priests of the established church. He steers clear of this opposition group. After causing Merlin's tower to crumble (because of the secret installation of some explosives), the Boss is hailed as an all-powerful purveyor of magic. With the help of a young man named Clarence, the Yankee begins to organize schools and factories to train workers for what he visualizes will be a superior society—perhaps a society like that in the late nineteenth century, but with less materialism and more dedication to intellectual and spiritual progress.

Challenged to a duel by Sir Sagramor, the Boss (accompanied by a young woman named Alisande—renamed "Sandy") goes on a tour of England. Two matters especially trouble him: the heaviness of his coat of mail, and the talkativeness of Sandy. Once in a while, he meets a man of more than usual intelligence; this man he sends back to Camelot, with a note addressed to Clarence. The man will become part of his Man-Factory. Hank comes to the castle of Morgan le Fay (King Arthur's jealous sister) and visits the dungeons under her castle. Against her wishes, he insists that all but one of the prisoners are to be released. In the Valley of Holiness, he repairs the broken wall of a deep well. When the water fills the well, masses of people agree that the Boss has worked another, wonderful "miracle." The Boss prophesies that King Arthur will soon visit the Valley of Holiness. (The Yankee knows of this visit, because Clarence tells him of it over a secretly installed telephone.) When King Arthur appears, the people declare that another miracle has been worked by the Boss. Finally, the king joins the Yankee (both in disguise), and the two secretly tour the countryside, surveying the true living conditions of the common people. King Arthur proves his courage and kindness when he personally helps care for some sick and starving peasants who have been excommunicated by the Church. The two travelers are captured and sold into slavery. In London, Hank maneuvers an escape, after picking the lock on his chains. A feature of the grand rescue is the arrival of Sir Launcelot and other knights—on bicycles.

Finally, the Yankee is forced to fight a duel with Sir Sagramor. The heavily-armored knight represents, not only himself and Merlin, but also all of the knights errant in England who are offended by the ideas of progress advanced by the Boss. The Yankee wears no armor—in fact, he is clad in tights. He continually ducks away from the lance of the charging Sir Sagramor and finally drags the knight to the ground with a lasso. Merlin steals the lasso, and (when Sir Sagramor again charges the Boss) the lightly dressed Yankee shoots the knight with a gun. All of the Knights of the Round Table assemble to charge the solitary Boss. He kills eleven of them with two guns, and he is relieved when the rest retreat—for he has only *one* more bullet.

A few years pass, and England is now reorganized along the lines of the industrial development of the late nineteenth century. The Yankee has married Sandy, and they have an infant daughter, named "Hello-Central." Returning to Camelot, after a trip to the seashore for the child's health, Hank finds King Arthur dead and the entire kingdom divided into two forces. The fight between King Arthur and Sir Launcelot has been over the king's wife, Queen Guenever. The established church has declared the "interdict"–excommunicating all those opposed to it. The masses of people who had once supported the Boss now flock back to the church. The Yankee and a small picked force of young men build a fortress surrounded by electrical wires. Most of the knights are killed in a grand attack, but the Boss is stabbed and then nursed by an old woman (Merlin, in disguise). Merlin casts a spell over the Yankee and states that he will sleep for thirteen hundred years. As the story ends, the Yankee awakens in the nineteenth century.

DETAILED SUMMARY OF

A CONNECTICUT YANKEE IN KING ARTHUR'S COURT

A WORD OF EXPLANATION

A "stranger" speaks to Mark Twain when the two men are being shown the wonders of Warwick Castle. The stranger talks softly but knowledgeably about the historic relics in the castle. At one point, their guide indicates a small hole in the chain-mail of a suit of armor. Mark Twain's companion, the stranger, mutters that he did it. Later, Twain glances around and finds that the mysterious stranger has disappeared. During the evening, the American author sits by the fire in his hotel room and reads a story from Sir Thomas Malory, describing an adventure of Sir Launcelot. Suddenly, there is a knock at the door and the stranger comes in and relates his story.

The stranger claims to be an American "born and reared in Hartford . . . Connecticut." He was head superintendent in an arms factory, and consequently knows a great deal about "guns, revolvers, cannons, boilers, engines . . . labor-saving machinery." One day during a misunderstanding ("conducted with crow-bars") with a worker named Hercules, the storyteller is hit over the head and completely blacks out. When the injured man awakens, he finds himself sitting under a tree in the middle of a country setting he has never seen before. A horseman, wearing some curious iron armor, questions the factory superintendent. The injured man innocently offends the man on the horse who retreats about six hundred feet and then comes rushing toward the factory worker. The horseman makes the superintendent his captive and the two men travel together to the town. The storyteller asks if they are nearing Bridgeport, Connecticut. The horseman replies that the name of the town is Camelot.

At this point, Twain's visitor seems to be very sleepy and so he offers leave a journal of his experiences. The American author takes the manuscript, which is "yellow with age." Sitting down by the fire, Mark Twain continues to read of the stranger's experiences. (He begins at the place in the story at which the man stopped describing his adventures. From this point, the entire narration is told from the point of view of the "Connecticut Yankee.")

CHAPTER 1

CAMELOT

The Yankee does not recognize Camelot as the name of any town that he knows. He assumes that, probably, it is the name of an insane asylum. He is quite surprised to see a young girl walk by him wearing a strange costume. He is even more surprised when a child notices him and appears very startled at his clothing. Finally, the horseman, wearing the armor, and the Yankee enter the town. The people "look like animals," with their "long, coarse, uncombed hair." The sound of "military music" is heard and a procession of horsemen, all dressed in armor, starts up the steep slopes of a hill, at the top of which is located at huge castle. Reaching the great gates of the castle, the procession (followed by the Yankee and his companion) crosses the draw bridge and is soon in a "great paved court."

CHAPTER 2

KING ARTHUR'S COURT

The Yankee questions several people to determine whether or not he is in an asylum. Finally, a "slim boy" approaches him and engages him in a conversation. The talkative boy mentions that he was born in the year 513. (At this point, the Yankee rapidly calculates that the boy must be nearly 1400 years old.) The boy (later called Clarence) announces that they are standing in King Arthur's Court and the date is June 19, 528. The Yankee is amazed. All at once, he remembers that on the 21st of June, 528, there was a total eclipse of the sun. He decides to reserve his opinion about the date of the year (528), until after the 21st of June. He decides, that if by chance, he is in the sixth century, then he has a head start—educationally of 1300 years over any man in the kingdom. Clarence tells the Yankee that he has been captured by Sir Kay. Hank is taken into a grand hall, in the midst of which is an "oaken table . . . called the Table Round." Dog fights frequently occur in the room, as bones are often thrown to the many dogs surrounding the eaters. In the room there are more than twenty prisoners, many of whom seem to be "suffering sharp physical pain."

CHAPTER 3

KNIGHTS OF THE TABLE ROUND

The people at the Round Table tell each other about their adventures. Evidently, they have participated in duels with strangers, rather than settling disputes or avenging injuries. The Yankee suspects that the knights are not very intellectual, but he notes that some of them are manly and that a few of them have "purity" reflected on their faces. Some of the prisoners kneel together and tell the queen (who is seated in the balcony) that they are her prisoners—"by command of Sir Kay." At the queen's look of disappointment, Sir Kay relates how Sir Launcelot, dressed in Sir Kay's armor, is the knight responsible for the prisoners. Queen Guenever is happy and embarrassed at the mention of Sir Launcelot. Clarence says to the Yankee that if Sir Kay had had a little more wine to drink, the story of the knight's accomplishments would be even more startling than it is. Then Merlin, a "very old and white-bearded man," tells a story—which evidently has been told many times before. Merlin's "droning voice" goes on and on while everyone takes a brief nap. His tale is about the time King Arthur received a sword from the Lady of the Lake.

CHAPTER 4

SIR DINADAN THE HUMORIST

At the conclusion of Merlin's tale, Sir Dinadan ties some of the metal cups to a dog's tail and turns him loose. The knight is proud of his "exploit," and the audience very much appreciates Sir Dinadan's cleverness. The "clever" knight makes a humorous speech. (The storyteller sadly remembers hearing the same worm-eaten jokes "1300 years afterward.") Then, Sir Kay rises and describes the tremendous battle he engaged in when he captured the Yankee. Sir Kay ends his tale by condemning the Yankee "to die at noon on the 21st." The Yankee is surprised at the indelicate language of the people of the court as they discuss his manner of death. Because the condemned man's clothing looks strange, and is suspected of being enchanted, his garments are removed. The Lords and Ladies stare unconcernedly at him. The only compliment the embarrassed Yankee receives on his naked appearance is the Queen's remark that she has never seen anyone with legs like that before. Finally, he is thrust into a dungeon.

CHAPTER 5

AN INSPIRATION

After having a good sleep, Hank awakens and is amused as he thinks of the "dream" that he has just had about being in the court of King Arthur. But Clarence appears and shatters the idea that it has just been a dream with the information that the Yankee is to "be burned to-morrow." When the Yankee expresses a strong desire to escape, he is told that Merlin "has woven a spell" about the dungeon. Clarence is sent to tell the king that the condemned man is also a magician. Clarence is very frightened at the thought that the Yankee may arrange a "calamity" that will upset King Arthur's court or cast an enchantment on his friend and impresses the King with his fears. Arthur is persuaded to release the Yankee until Merlin convinces him not to on the grounds that the Yankee has not named the "calamity" and is probably bluffing. When Clarence returns with the news, the Yankee remembers that the eclipse of the 21st might offer him an occasion to trick the superstitious minds. The Yankee sends word by Clarence to the king that he intends, at the hour appointed for the burning, to "smother the whole world in the dead blackness of midnight." Clarence faints.

CHAPTER 6

THE ECLIPSE

While Hank is thinking about how clever he is, the door of his dungeon cell opens. He is told that his execution has been "set forward a day." Horrified, the Yankee is taken to the court. Clarence slips to his side and explains that the shift in date has been made because he (Clarence) had it moved forward. (The boy believes that the Yankee can save himself with magic, and so he is very anxious to have the condemned man start to prove his abilities at the earliest opportunity. Four thousand people breathlessly watch as the Yankee is bound to a stake and little sticks are piled high about his body, while a man kneels at his feet "with a blazing torch" and a monk starts to pray in Latin. All at once, the eclipse (expected on the next day) begins. Taking advantage of the situation, the Yankee poses in a "grand" manner, with his arm stretching up pointing to the sun. King Arthur reasons with the Yankee. He says: "Name any terms . . . but banish this calamity, spare the sun!" At this point, Hank finds out that the day *is* the 21st of June—the day of the expected eclipse. Clarence had not told him the correct date previously. While the eclipse is going through its cycle, the Yankee bargains with the king, insisting that he be next to the king in power. Stalling until the eclipse passes, the Yankee asks for suitable clothing for one of his new rank. By the time he is suitably clothed, everything is pitch-dark. The Yankee knows that at any moment the eclipse will go through the second half of its phase and that, gradually, there will be more and more light. So, the Yankee lifts up his hand and says: "Let the enchantment dissolve and pass harmless away!" At this moment, a tiny sliver of light shines out of the sky. The Yankee is victorious.

COMMENT ("A Word of Explanation"—Chapter 6): Mark Twain uses the Gothic device of having someone tell him the story, the general idea being to make the reader feel that everything really happened. The "curious stranger" is the storyteller (Hank Morgan—the Yankee). The "round hole in the chain-mail in the left breast" (of the armor of the knight Sir Sagramor le Desirous) is curiously explained, when the stranger says: *"I saw it done* . . . I did it myself." The idea of the time sequence in the novel is suggested early, when the stranger refers to the "transposition of epochs—and bodies." "The Stranger's History" takes the reader part way into the sixth century by means of the oral storytelling; but, before the chapter is concluded, the reader is back in Mark Twain's room, as Twain begins to read the stranger's manuscript (made of "parchment, and yellow with age"). Thus, almost the entire story is made up of what Twain reads from the manuscript. The "I" in the tale is the Yankee—Hank Morgan, later called the "Boss."

The time of the beginning of the story is established, in Chapter 1, as being June 19, 528. (The Yankee leaves Connecticut in 1879, the year of the publication of the novel.) The picture of Merlin is the standard literary one of a "very old and white bearded man, clothed in a flowering black grown,"—although Twain makes him out to seem rather silly at times, as when he gestures wildly with his hands. Twain refers to Merlin's long tale during which everyone takes a nap) as a "quaint lie"—a satirical poke at mediaeval romances. In Chapter 4, Twain suggests that Sir Walter Scott's characters (Rebecca, Rowena, and Ivanhoe) would use language which would shock people in modern days—but Scott put polite conversation into their mouths. In Chapter 5, Twain satirically indicates that the lying magician "Merlin" exists in all times and places (such as Egypt or India), but he goes under a variety of names, including Smith, Jones, and Robinson. Note the chiaroscura (contrast in light and dark) in Chapter 6, when the Yankee is taken from the "darkness" of his dungeon cell to the "fierce glare of daylight." Finally, observe that Hank, displaying Yankee ingenuity, adapts himself to the pace of the eclipse as it progresses. His timing is perfect as he says dramatically: "Let the enchantment dissolve and pass harmless away!"—and the edge of the sun is again seen.

CHAPTER 7

MERLIN'S TOWER

Dressed in rich clothing, the Yankee is now the "second personage in the kingdom." He is surprised that he does not find many of the "conveniences" of the nineteenth century–such as soap, matches, or looking-glasses. He feels as if he were "another Robinson Crusoe cast away on an uninhabited island." But people are fascinated with their new leader; many times a day he has to show himself to the people who travel miles to look at him. Because Hank was so successful with one miracle (the eclipse of the sun), people began to ask for another. Merlin spreads rumors that the Yankee is a "humbug," so the Yankee throws Merlin into prison. With the help of Clarence, the Yankee prepares a "miracle." The two secretly place blasting powder among the stones of Merlin's Tower, and attached to a lightning rod are wires running to the powder. On the appointed day crowds watch, waiting to witness the Yankee's miracle. Finally, the sky darkens and the Yankee knows that there is soon to be a thunder storm. Merlin is encouraged to protect his tower. The old man mutters to himself and makes motions in the air with his hands. Then, at the proper moment, the Yankee moves his hands about in the air and the stones of the tower leap "into the sky in chunks." Hank has fortunately seen a sliver of lightning head toward the lightning rod. His miracle is a sure thing) Merlin loses face, and the king wants to "stop his wages . . . even . . . to banish him." The Yankee says that perhaps Merlin could be helpful in small matters requiring magic. Merlin does not thank the Yankee, for he is irritated that his place at the Court of King Arthur has been usurped.

CHAPTER 8

THE BOSS

After the Yankee destroys Merlin's Tower, his power as the new minister is solidified. At first, Hank awakens in the mornings thinking that his living in Arthur's court is only a dream. Finally, he accepts the thought that he is now living in the sixth century. Although the Yankee's power is "equal to the king," he is upset that the church is stronger than both the king and the minister. The Yankee is surprised that the people seem to be wholly subservient towards their king and church and nobility. To one used to nineteenth-century freedom, their rabbit-like attitudes are pitiful. Most of the people "of King Arthur's British nation" are slaves who refuse to recognize that fact. The Yankee considers himself "A giant among pygmies, a man among children"; the only man in the realm with a spirit of independence. One day a blacksmith refers to the Connecticut Yankee as "The Boss" and he likes the new title.

CHAPTER 9

THE TOURNAMENT

At Camelot, there are numerous tournaments. (These seem to resemble county fairs of the nineteenth and twentieth centuries.) Crowds gather and watch with eagerly, with a happy-hearted "indifference to morals" while a knight is pierced with a spear ("lance") by an opponent. The Boss attends all of these tournaments, and in addition, has a member of his staff write reports about them. (The articles, which the Boss wants to develop into a newspaper, resemble long winded reports in a medieval romance.) Hank sits in his private box and talks with one of the contestants—who tells "humorous" jokes which many centuries later once bothered the Yankee. The Boss is so irritated at the jokester, that he says aloud: "I hope to gracious he is killed! Another knight thinks that the Boss is referring to him. At the end of the tournament the angry knight, Sir Sagramor, tells the Boss that there is a "little account to settle between" them—and suggests a "day three or four years in the future" when the two men might fight each other. Sir Sagramor then leaves to search for the Holy Grail.

CHAPTER 10

BEGINNINGS OF CIVILIZATION

When King Arthur hears of Sir Sagramor's challenge, the Boss is told that he should "set forth in quest of adventures." But

Hank is too busy organizing people and activities to "take a holiday." The Boss is afraid of the established church for he is trying to revamp the feudal society, and has brought together "the brightest young minds" he could find to train under his guidance. He has begun a "teacher-factory" and many Sunday schools where religion is one's individual choice. After four years, the Boss has the "civilization of the nineteenth century booming. However, the "civilization" is "fenced away from the public view," for the Boss is afraid that he will be opposed by the Church. He also secretly has a military academy and a naval academy. Clarence (now 22 years old) is his "right hand man," and has been trained for journalism. There is a telegraph and a telephone system installed although they are only "for private service . . . as yet." At this time King Arthur reminds the Boss that four years earlier the minister had promised to go on a quest when everything was properly organized. So, Hank is faced with the problem of getting himself hoisted on a horse and "starting out to seek adventures."

CHAPTER 11

THE YANKEE IN SEARCH OF ADVENTURE

To King Arthur's Round Table come many people who tell strange and tall tales. One day, a young woman tells about her mistress who is a "captive in a vast and gloomy castle, along with forty-four other young and beautiful girls, pretty much all of them princesses." For twenty-six years three stupendous brothers, each with four arms and one eye, "have been masters of the castle." All the knights clamor for the chance to rescue the maidens but King Arthur tells the Boss that this is his "opportunity for adventure." The unenthusiastic Boss talks with the woman who first describes the captives. Her name is "the Demoiselle Alisande la Carteloise"—rechristined by the Boss as Sandy. It seems that Sandy's story has been believed by everyone without benefit of proof. When the Boss questions her as to the location of the castle, she confuses him with roundabout directions. Clarence observes that the Boss will have no difficulty in finding the castle, for Sandy will accompany him on the adventure. After eating an early breakfast and enduring much suffering getting packed into his armor, Hank is lifted numbly onto his horse, and Sandy takes her place behind him. He is ready for the grand adventure.

CHAPTER 12

SLOW TORTURE

The world surounding the Boss, Sandy and her horse is a very beautiful world. But another world is much nearer the Boss, and this is not such a beautiful world. This latter world is made up of the space between the body of the Boss and his armor. After a little while, he wants to get a handkerchief to wipe his brow, but he cannot reach it–for it is in his helmet, which has been screwed on. Inside his armor, Hank rattles "like a crate of dishes." He begins to feel as if he were about "to get fried" in his metal armor. Suddenly a fly enters through the bars of the helmet. The fly performs a dance, as it steps lightly from the Boss's nose to his lip–from his lip to his ear. Finally, Sandy takes off the helmet and fills it with water. The Yankee drinks, and then Sandy pours the rest of the water "down inside the armor." Sandy is a very good-natured woman, but her "flow of talk" is "as steady as a mill."

CHAPTER 13

FREEMEN

No self-respecting knight takes food with him, for he would look ridiculous with a "basket of sandwiches . . . hanging . . . on his spear." During the first night the Boss and Sandy each slip under a separate rug. There is no one to help the Boss take his armor off, so he keeps it on. Not only does he become cold, he is also the focal point for the "bugs and ants and worms" which "flock in out of the wet and crawl down inside" the armor "to get warm." The Boss is irritated by the procession of ants, which parade up and down his body. In the morning, Hank is in a sad condition, but the nobly born Sandy is "as fresh as a squirrel" being rather used to primitive living. Before sunrise, the two adventurers start off–"Sandy riding" and the Boss "limping along behind." Sandy is scornful when the Boss proposes to have breakfast with some freemen who are mending the roads. The Yankee comments against the established church which has perpetuated the chattel status of these people. Only one man struggles to understand the position taken by the Boss. The Yankee writes instructions to Clarence to give this man a place in the "Man-Factory" at Camelot.

CHAPTER 14

"DEFEND THEE, LORD"

Because the Boss gives the freemen "three pennies" for his breakfast they make him a gift of a flint and steel. After the Boss lights his pipe, a blast of smoke shoots out "through the bars" of his helmet. The people flee in fright from the seeming-dragon. Even Sandy talks less than usual when they start off until she overcomes her awe of the pipe. When "half a dozen armed knights" charge toward the Yankee, he waits until they get in front of him, and then he puffs white smoke through the bars of the helmet again. The six knights run away, but they stop several hundred yards away. Sandy tells him that they are waiting to give themselves up to him and then talks to the knights and tells them that the victor is the Boss, the legendary second-in-command. The knights are sworn "to appear at Arthur's court within two days." From this time on they will be knights of the Boss and under his command.

CHAPTER 15

SANDY'S TALE

The Boss and Sandy leave the knights who are to report to King Arthur's court. Sandy starts spinning a long, rambling tale of knights (Sir Gawaine and Sir Uwaine who have many adventures.) Sandy talks on and on and on, and the Boss once in a while, when not sleeping, listens in on her story. He interrupts her at intervals with comments calculated to shorten her drifting story. She answers his questions briefly and then, happily, goes on with her story—just as if he has not spoken. They approach a castle, strange to Sandy, located high on a hill.

COMMENT (Chapters 7-15): Notice Twain's satirical description of mediaeval tapestries: "a picture . . . the size of a bedquilt . . . woven or knitted," with "darned places in it" but nothing is the "right color or the right shape." In the beginning of Chapter 8, the "dream" Hank has is much like the "dream" both boys have in Twain's *The Prince and the Pauper.* One of Twain's primary targets is the established church. Hank is given the title "the Boss" by a blacksmith. In chapter 9, the priest's newspaper description of a tournament is satirically directed towards mediaeval romance. Chapter 10 is filled with details suggesting an industrial "Utopia"—as visualized by the Boss. The Yankee has spent four years in King Arthur's England up to this point (Chapter 10). Sandy (in Chapter 11) is given an almost endless sentence (called a "Run-On Sentence") beginning with "Oh, please you sir," where Twain again satirizes the mediaeval romance. Parts of the Boss' armor were his "greaves" (armor for the leg below the knee) and "cuisses" (defensive plate armor for the thighs, especially in front). Chapter 12 is a burlesque of mediaeval knights traveling in their cumbersome armor. Chapter 13 refers to Twain's great admiration for the French Revolution, which he calls "ever memorable and blessed." In the same chapter is a fine reference to "clothes philosophy." (See Essay Question 1, in section titled "Essay Questions for Answers and Review.") Also in Chapter 13 is a reference to John Locke's political philosophy that men have *"at all times* an undeniable . . . right *to alter their form of government* in such a manner as they may think expedient." Twain says the people need "a new deal" —the basis of Franklin Roosevelt's slogan in the 1930's. Note the doubleplay in Chapter 15, as Sandy tells an endless story while the Boss questions her throwing in his own interpretations of her dialogue, plus his own wanderin thought associations.

CHAPTER 16

MORGAN LE FAY

As the Yankee and Sandy approach the castle, a knight rides up to them. In place of his shield is a square piece of hard material which he wears attached to his arm. On this material is a sign: "Persimmons's Soap—All The Prime-Donne Use It." (The Yankee has all the knights under his charge carrying signs advertising different products—particularly those concerned with cleanliness.) The castle belongs to Morgan le Fay, the sister of King Arthur. Her husband is old King Uriens, the kind but subdued monarch of a tiny kingdom. Eventually, the two travelers are admitted to the castle where they are entertained by "Mrs. le Fay." While Morgan le Fay is being a most gracious and entertaining hostess, a servant slips and falls lightly against her. Casually, she slips a dagger into him. This does not dismay the Boss who has heard of her malevolent nature and her black deeds awed by the whole realm. During the interview the Boss lets drop a complimentary word about King Arthur. (He has forgotten that almost everybody knows how Morgan le Fay hates her brother, King Arthur.) Immediately, she cries out: "Hale me these varlets to the dungeons." Sandy then tells the queen that she is speaking of "the Boss." At once, Morgan le Fay becomes charming as before and says that she is jesting.

CHAPTER 17

A ROYAL BANQUET

The Boss notes that the sixth-century nobility are "morally rotten . . . but . . . enthusiastically religious." Nothing could deter the most murderous noble from attending divine service five or more times daily. During the banquet, a band, located in a gallery high in the air, plays the first version of what later came to be known as "In the Sweet Bye and Bye." (The queen is displeased with the musical number, and orders the composer hanged after dinner.) After an hour and half of heavy eating, gallons of wine and mead are consumed which leads to the exchange of many daring anecdotes. An old woman leaning upon a crutch, curses the queen and Morgan majetically sends her to the stake. Sandy is again inspired and tells Morgan le Fay that she must take back the command—or the Boss "will dissolve the castle and it shall vanish away like . . . a dream!" (This is a test to determine how much the queen fears Hank.) Morgan humbly recalls her command. Proudly, the Boss is escorted to the dungeons of the castle where he sees a man on a rack (a mechanical device, devised to torture a person by stretching his arms and his legs.) On the rack is a "young giant of thirty" years of age named Hugo. The young man will not confess that he is guilty of killing a stag (deer), for if he does, after he is killed, all of his few possessions will be taken by the law, and his wife and children will be beggers. The Boss has Hugo released much to the relief of his anguished wife who sits holding their child in a corner of the dungeon. The Boss determines to have brave Hugo and his faithful wife as part of his colony where he is going to "turn groping and grubbing automata into *men.*"

CHAPTER 18

IN THE QUEEN'S DUNGEONS

After making arrangements to send Hugo to the "Factory," the Boss tries to think of some suitable punishment for the man who was stretching Hugo's limbs on the rack. Finally, the happy idea occurs to the Yankee that the executioner should be made "leader of the band." (This will insure that his torturer will soon be punished, for he cannot play a note of music.) Morgan le Fay, a little afraid the Boss will hold her latest murder against her, boasts that she intends to "*pay*" the relatives of the young page she killed with the dagger. According to law, she had a right to kill the boy but did not have to justify herself or make amends afterwards. Morgan takes the Yankee on a tour of her dungeons, where he is impressed with the sight of a man and a woman, both imprisoned for nine years in separate cells. They have entered the dungeons on the night of their wedding, and each has aged dreadfully. When Hank has them brought face to face they briefly glance at each other and then can only look toward the floor—their lovely romance has withered along with their bodies. Forty-seven persons are released from the dungeons. One man had been imprisoned because he once said that Morgan le Fay had red hair. He should have said that her hair was "auburn." Five prisoners have been such a long time in the dungeons that no one remembers why they were placed there. One prisoner is there for the crime of stating his belief that men were all equal; the Boss sends him along to the Factory.

CHAPTER 19

KNIGHT-ERRANTRY AS A TRADE

After two days and two nights in Morgan le Fay's corrupting presence, the Boss is happy to leave. Again, Sandy starts on her long tale of knights and their adventures. The Boss cannot understand how evil Morgan le Fay is able to present a "fresh and young" appearance to the world. For almost the first time during the excursion, Sandy has nothing to say when the Boss asks her, "How old are you, Sandy?"

CHAPTER 20

THE OGRE'S CASTLE

After traveling ten miles, the travelers meet a knight who wears a sign attached over the breast plate of his armor. The Boss recognizes the knight as Sir Madok de la Montaine, for his sign reads: "Use Peterson's Prophylactic Tooth-Brush–All The Go." On Sir Madok's shield is a motto, "Try Noyoudont"–an advertisement for a "tooth-wash" introduced by the Boss. Sir Madok is angry, for one of his fellow knights (the jokester, Sir Ossaise of Surluse) recently told him where he might find some customers who would appreciate his advertisements. After much inconvenience, Sir Madok finds he has been directed toward five very old people who have not had a tooth among them for twenty years. Finally, the Boss and his guide approach what she calls "the castle." The Yankee sees nothing but a pigsty. Sandy explains to him that what she sees is the real thing, but that he is seeing falsely–for he is enchanted. Philosophically, the Boss accepts her explanation. The pigs at the pigsty are the Princesses, (the damsels in distress). The "ogres" are three humble swine-herds. For "sixteen pennies," the Boss buys the freedom of the "damsels." The old sow of the lot is addressed by Sandy as "my Lady" and "your Highness." The Boss and Sandy take the damsels over ten miles of country to the place Sandy designates as their home. Naturally, the "Princesses" are installed in the house which begins to smell curiously like a pigsty.

CHAPTER 21

THE PILGRIMS

The Boss believes that Sandy's strange idea about the identity of the pigs are because of her "training . . . influence . . . education." To doubt enchantments in the sixth century would be the same as doubting the existence of the telephone in the nineteenth century. In the morning the swine are sent their breakfast with ceremony, while Sandy and the Boss eat at the servant's table. The Boss inquires where the owners of the house are. (The owners have not appeared since the pigs arrived.) Sandy does not understand why he bothers to ask this question for the owner of the house should be honored to have the "Princesses" as his distinguished guests. The Boss thinks he is now going to rid himself of Sandy for he believes that she will want to stop and watch over the Princesses," but she disappoints him when she says that she will not leave him until some "champion" shall win her from him. Before the Boss and Sandy leave, he gives the "whole peerage" ("The Princesses") to the servants. The two travelers start out on their journey and, eventually, join a merry "procession of pilgrims." Among the rough stories tossed back and forth among the pilgrims is a tale about some monks who bathed themselves in a miraculous fountain, but their impurities caused it to dry up. In the afternoon another procession is met, but the people in this group are ragged slaves. They are chained together and have traveled 300 miles in eighteen days. The "trader" in charge of them rides his horse up and down the line of fifty people and whips them if they lag from weariness. One woman with child starts to fall and men-slaves are forced to hold her while she is lashed with the whip. The Boss and Sandy, accompanying the first procession of pilgrims, leave the band of slaves. One of the Yankee's knights (Sir Ozana le Cure Hardy) rides up and announces to the group that the "miraculous fountain toward which they ride has dried up." Merlin (a magician and the Boss's arch enemy) is trying his "magic" to recover the flow of the water, however, the Boss's efforts are needed. So the Yankee issues instructions back to Clarence to send some chemicals to the fountain in the Valley of Holiness.

CHAPTER 22

THE HOLY FOUNTAIN

Many Pilgrims have come to the Valley of Holiness. They discover that the water at the shrine has stopped flowing. However, instead of going home immediately, they stay around to get a look at "the place where it . . . used to be." The holy community is made up of a number of buildings, including a monastery (for the men) and a nunnery (for the women). Merlin has been busily attempting to "bring . . . the water back again." The Boss decides that he will let Merlin thoroughly demonstrate his inability to perform a miracle– then he (the Boss), will perform a scientific "miracle" and bring the water back. Hank has himself lowered into the well, where he finds a hole in the wall. (The water has been rising to the position in the well where the hole is located, and then running off underground somewhere.) The Yankee spreads the news around that what he is about to do is very difficult. He realizes that he cannot perform his "miracle" until the supplies arrive, which he earlier instructed Clarence to send. So, the Yankee bides his time by allowing Merlin to continue with his miracle. The Yankee and Sandy wander about looking at hermits who live near the holy fountain. All are dirty, and most of them have placed their bodies in strange positions, which attracts public attention. One of the outstanding hermits stands on top of a "pillar sixty feet high, with a broad platform on the top of it." All day long, he bows his body toward the ground and the sky, back and forth. (Later, the Boss attaches some cords to him, using the hermit's movements to run a sewing machine.) Visiting pilgrims stand in reverent awe of these vermin-laden dignitaries, envious of their "pious austerities."

CHAPTER 23

RESTORATION OF THE FOUNTAIN

Merlin continues to burn smoke-powders, to paw the air with his hands, and to mutter strange words, but his miracle is slow in coming. Finally, Merlin says to the abbot of the monastery: "the water will flow no more forever, good Father. I have done what man could. Suffer me to go." Now the Yankee's time has arrived. He sets up a few "conditions"—he insists that the area around the well be vacated for a half a mile. After a time, the experts sent by Clarence arrive in the Valley of Holiness, and the Boss is able to commence with his elaborate "miracle." First of all, he has the leak in the well mended. (The water immediately begins to rise.) He attaches a "little iron pump" to a "section of lead pipe" extending from the well to the door of the chapel. Then, he places fire rockets in a large barrel on the roof of the chapel. Finally, he has built a high, beautifully decorated platform. Since "one can't throw too much style into a miracle." Hordes of people pour into the valley to watch. Even Merlin is there. The Boss has a solemn stage-wait for about twenty minutes. Then he stands on the platform, with his face turned toward Heaven, all the time holding his hands out towards the audience. He slowly pronounces a long made-up germanic word. This is followed by a blue light from a flare touched off by an electrical connection. The Boss then utters a still longer word, and then a red flare goes off. After his next word and green flares, for a mighty climax, he spreads his arms out and thunders his final awe-inspiring syllables. This is followed by a rainbow of flares, effectively accompanied by bursting rockets. At this moment the water is seen coming from the lead pipe. The people are thrilled, and Merlin is overcome. The Yankee is looked upon as "some kind of a supreme being." He has established for himself a tremendous "reputation" as a magician.

CHAPTER 24

A RIVAL MAGICIAN

About this time the Boss decides that he would like to abolish the idea that bathing is immoral and has the ruins of an old bath rebuilt. What he ends up with is "a spacious pool of clear pure water that a body could swim in." The abbot is persuaded to take the first bath. The Yankee catches a bad cold, and Sandy nurses him which exhausts her. Leaving her to rest the Boss walks up into the hills and finds a cave, known to be the den of a famous hermit. To his surprise, he finds that the cave has been turned into a telephone office. Yankee talks with

Clarence back at Camelot and learns that the king and queen are just starting out towards the Valley of Holiness. When Hank gets back to the monastery, he finds that a new magician has arrived. The specialty of this celebrity from Asia is to relate what people throughout the world are doing "at the moment." The Yankee notices that no one questions the new magician's announcements. The Boss asks the magician to explain what he (the Boss) is doing with his right hand. The magician is ill at ease, but he finally says that he only speaks of the "doings of . . . kings, princes, emperors." To prove his point, he explains what King Arthur is doing–he claims that the king is sleeping, tired from the hunt. The Boss says the king is riding. The new magician claims that Arthur and his court are headed "toward the sea." The Boss says that Arthur and his court will be in the Valley of Holiness soon. The Boss is somewhat irritated that people seem to believe the new magician rather than him. (He has just performed a mighty "miracle," and people seem to be forgetting it.) The king and the court do arrive, and the abbot of the monastery is angry and humiliated, because there has been no preparation for the visit. The Asian celebrity has been disproved as a magician, and the "reputation" of the Boss is "in the sky again."

COMMENT (Chapters 16-24): Twain ridicules "knight errant" by having them traveling around advertising soap products (Chapter 16). The episode involving Hugo dramatically underscores the unjust laws of the day. Morgan le Fay is described by a vivid metaphor: she is a "Vesuvius." Chapter 20 states dramatically that "all revolutions that will succeed must *begin* in blood." (This is much like Twain's earlier comment on the French Revolution, in Chapter 13.) The enchantment in Chapter 20 is much like Don Quixote's "enchantments" (or misinterpretations of objects in Cervante's *Don Quixote*.) Notice Twain's satire on human indifference to suffering, as he has a group of religious "pilgrims" calmly and casually observe a group of slaves being whipped (in Chapter 21). In Chapter 22, Twain pokes fun at religious pilgrimages (perhaps also the revivalist camp meetings of his own day?), as he pictures feasting and drinking in the Valley of Holiness. Sandy enjoys speaking one long "Run-On Sentence" (in Chapter 22) which both the Boss and a typical reader find difficult to understand. Twain's own dramatic lecture technique is illustrated (in Chapter 23), as he discusses the effect of expectancy on audiences. In Chapter 24 is a description of the basis of some of Twain's own (literary) comic effects, as he describes a "jumbling together of extravagant incongruities" and a "fantastic conjunction of opposites and irreconcilables." (This technique is elsewhere explained in more detail in an essay, entitled "How to Tell a Story.")

CHAPTER 25

A COMPETITIVE EXAMINATION

King Arthur decides to tour through the kingdom in disguise, accompanied by the Boss. However, before he starts on his trip, as Chief Justice of the King's Bench, he has to render some decisions. All of his decisions seem to favor the aristocracy. For example, he allows a young orphan girl's property removed from her and given to the Church. The Boss is surprised at what seems to be King Arthur's lack of justice, but he realizes that Arthur is governing according to his background of experience. Next, candidates wishing to be officers come in front of an Examining Board. The Yankee is overcome with shame and indignation to find that only the "well-born folk" are selected to be officers—even though they know nothing of war. All the men who have been privately trained by the Boss are refused the opportunity to be officers—for, though they know much about war, they cannot fulfill the rule requiring four generations of nobility. The Yank proposes a regiment made up entirely of officers. In this way, he can keep the members of the nobility together and people the rest of the army with nobodies chosen merely on the basis of efficiency.

CHAPTER 26

THE FIRST NEWSPAPER

The Boss notices that King Arthur does not feel that he has to tell his queen (Guenever) when he is going on a trip around the country. (The queen has her mind on Sir Launcelot.) King Arthur holds a special kind of court. All of eight hundred sick people are individually treated by the king who rubs their sores and then gives each one a coin. The king's touch is supposed to cure their sickness. (Many of these people appear to be more interested in the coins than the cure. While in the past the coin has been gold, the Yankee makes coins out of nickel—allowing the kingdom to save money. After the ceremony has been going on for three hours, the Boss, feeling bored, is thrilled by a news boy (the very first ever) hawking the *"Camelot Weekly Hosannah and Literary Volcano."* The first edition of the Boss's newspaper has many proofreading errors, but, by and large, he is pleased with it. The monks do not understand what the paper is, and the Boss explains that it is meant to be read, not worn. The monks are amazed and the Yankee, tremendously proud of his latest creation, accepts the eloquent compliments without a trace of modesty.

CHAPTER 27

THE YANKEE AND THE KING TRAVEL INCOGNITO

The Boss cuts King Arthur's hair so they can ride through the country disguised as poor persons. The two men leave on their travels, and cover about ten miles quickly. While the Boss is getting some water for the monarch to drink, "people of quality" approach the king who looks as humble as the "leaning tower at Pisa." A servant at the end of the procession raises a whip and, realizing that the King of England would not submit to a whipping, the Boss jumps in time to arrive under the whip lash. Sometime later the two men discuss the phenomenon of prophecy. The Boss explains that to foretell the far-distant future is easy—for no one can check on the information. At one point during the walk the king is almost run over by some knights on horseback. He moves out of their way just in time and then, with royal enthusiasm, curses them. The two furious knights turn the horses and start for the king. Hank tries to save the royal hide by tossing out a barrage of insults which makes the king's cursing "seem pure and cheap by comparison." The knights naturally turn their horses and start for the Boss who tosses a bomb he has been saving for just such an emergency.

CHAPTER 28

DRILLING THE KING

The Boss realizes that the king cannot travel incognito while he feels and acts like a member of royalty, so the Boss drills the king. King Arthur walks around, practicing slouching his shoulders and looking oppressed. The addition of a knapsack makes him look even more humble. But the Boss realizes that all of his coaching will not educate the king the way actual experience will. They prepare to visit the hut of some very poor people.

CHAPTER 29

THE SMALLPOX HUT

There seemed to be no one about the hut. When the travelers enter a woman asks them to be merciful, saying "all is taken, nothing is left." King Arthur goes to get some water for the woman who is dying of smallpox. The Boss tries to warn the king away from the sick woman, but the king insists that it would be a shame if he did not help. He considers his "knightly honor [to be] at stake here." The woman asks the king to climb the ladder which goes toward the loft and look about upstairs. The king returns with the body of a young girl who is almost dead with smallpox; the woman's husband is already dead near her. Then the woman explains that her three sons were wrongly blamed for cutting down some fruit trees. The woman and her husband had to labor with the harvest, to take the place of the sons. The harvest of the family was neglected while the family gathered the lord's harvest. Then they were heavily taxed by the Church and the lord. In despair, the woman cursed the Church and the entire family was excommunicated. The few remaining members of the family are dying of smallpox, shunned by the neighbors who could aid them but who are in horror of "the curse of Rome."

CHAPTER 30

THE TRAGEDY OF THE MANOR-HOUSE

By midnight, all of the family are dead. As the king and the Boss leave the hut, they hear the three sons (who have escaped prison) knock on the door seeking their parents. The two travelers hurry away. The king is annoyed because the three sons (guilty or not) have escaped "their lord." He could still understand only the viewpoint of "quality" people and could not conceive of justice in terms of the peasants. They see a fire in the distance and upon approaching, a number of dead bodies hanging from limbs of trees. The Boss and King Arthur hide in the bushes until the excitement is over. Then they ask for hospitality at a hut. The wife explains that the manor house of Abblasoure has burned. All the noble family were located and saved—except for the "master," who is eventually found killed, in the bushes. Various people are suspected, and eighteen are hanged or butchered. The husband of the woman who tells about the fire has helped hang and butcher the suspects. In a conversation with the husband the Yankee discovers that the man has been helping to seem in sympathy with the killed "master." When the Boss explains that he does not feel any sympathy for the "master," the man says that he agrees with the Boss.

CHAPTER 31

MARCO

The Boss and the king stroll leisurely along. Suddenly, they are startled by a shrieking group of boys and girls, who have been "imitating their elders . . . playing mob": they are hanging a little boy. The two travelers rescue the child. They continue on until they come to a small town where the Boss is pleased to see his new coins in circulation, replacing the primitive barter system used before. He proves to Marco, a friendly villager, and the other townspeople that he is an important man by asking for change "for a twenty-dollar gold piece." The Boss wants to please Marco, and so he suggests that Marco give a party at his house for some of his friends and neighbors.

Thoughtfully, the Boss adds: "You must also allow me to pay the costs." The Boss makes believe that "Jones" (the fictitious name for King Arthur) wants to do a favor for Marco and suggests that Marco would not want "to offend" "Jones" by not accepting the favor. The Boss goes to the local store and orders a great quantity of foods and furnishings to be delivered to Marco's house.

CHAPTER 32

DOWLEY'S HUMILIATION

The "Boss" reminds King Arthur that his Majesty is to make-believe he is a farmer for the benefit of the townspeople. At the party, one of the guests, Dowley the blacksmith relates the secret of his success, bragging endlessly. The other members of the party are admiring of him and support his extravagant claims of prosperity. While Dowley boasts, Marco's wife begins to prepare the meal. First, she brings out a new table which she covers with a sparkling tablecloth. (Dowley is beginning to be curious.) Next, the good lady brings out two new stools—then two more—and then two more. Her husband quietly says: "leave the rest." The sight of all this new wealth is staggering. In quick succession, Mrs. Marco brings out new dishes and a wide variety of foods. At this point, the storekeeper's son comes with the bill, which amounts to "thirty-nine thousand one hundred and fifty milrays." Dowley was able to support his family of three in high style for a cost of sixty-nine cents, two mils, and six milrays a year. The Boss pays the boy four dollars, and he tells him to keep the change. Dowley, the braggard, collapses.

CHAPTER 33

SIXTH-CENTURY POLITICAL ECONOMY

The Boss has now captured the "reverence" of Dowley, who believes the Boss to be very rich. In this feudal land only a man's rank or fortune won respect for him. His intellect and character were irrelevant. The Boss works the conversation around to the discussion of wages. It seems that Dowley pays his employees twice the amount workers are paid back at Camelot. But food in Dowley's area costs twice what it does in Camelot. The Boss faces the smith with the thought that the high wages are not *really* higher in fact, because the cost of living is higher. Annoyed that Dowley cannot see his point, the clever Yankee illustrates economic reality by demonstrating that real wages are proved by the amount of goods one is able to purchase in exchange for his productive effort. After all the arguments are presented, Dowley proudly tells the Boss that wages where he lives are higher. Frustrated, the Yankee is angry that he cannot reason with this ignorant country blacksmith and plans to get even with Dowley. Dowley had bragged that he paid a worker higher than usual wages. The irritated Yankee reminds Dowley that if a "master shall venture . . . to pay anything" more than the standard wage, he "shall be both fined and pilloried for it." Again, Dowley collapses—this time with the fear of death in his eyes. (He knows that to be pilloried might well be the death of him.)

CHAPTER 34

THE YANKEE AND THE KING SOLD AS SLAVES

While the Boss and Dowley have been discussing economics, the king has been taking a nap. Refreshed, King Arthur joins the Yankee who is beginning to regret his ragging of Dowley. They are strangers, and Marco and his friends probably believe that the unlawful payment of wages will be reported to the authorities. When the king (pretending to be a farmer) starts to ramble on about farming activities, the mob grows increasingly restless. The peasants, in a gesture of self-defense, suddenly throw themselves upon the two men, shouting: "Kill them!" Taking advantage of the peasants' state of panic which has almost blinded them, the king and the Yankee escape. They dash through the woods toward a stream of water, which they wade through until they find a huge branch of an oak "sticking out over the water." They work themselves along this branch and into the tree. After a time, the farmers arrive with their dogs, who lead their masters to the wrong tree. As luck would have it, the man chosen to climb the tree, accidentally mistakes his way and starts climbing the right tree. There is a fight in the tree, and King Arthur and the Boss are soon smoked out. The unexpected arrival of a gentleman and his retinue stops the battle and disperses the mob. The gentleman (Lord Grip) kindly supplies the two with horses and they continue their journey with their rescuer. But upon entering the lord's town sometimes later, they are suddenly handcuffed together and sold as slaves in the marketplace. The crowning humiliation comes when the Boss is sold for two dollars more than the king.

> **COMMENT (Chapters 25-34):** The Boss realizes that King Arthur favors ignorant, nobly born youth over educated poor ones. (Is Twain satirizing the right to vote statutes when he writes in Chapter 25 of a court regulation "requiring four generations of nobility or else the candidate is not eligible"?) Chapter 26 is an excellent satire and comic chapter on small town newspapers. (The conduct of King Arthur, in Chapter 27 is parallel with the conduct of the disguised King Edward in *The Prince and the Pauper.*) King Arthur's true sense of nobility is illustrated as he helps poor people in the smallpox hut. In chapter 30, the talkative woman who inquires of the "terrible goings-on at the manor house of Abblasoure" is reminiscent of Judith Loftus (the woman who questions Huck) in *Huck Finn.* In Chapter 31, Twain vividly paints a picture of a mob of boys and girls who imitate their elders in hanging a little fellow. Chapter 32 offers some good comedy, when the Marco family displays its new wealth–*more* than "keeping up with the Joneses." Chapter 32 offers a very detailed argument concerning the objective purchasing power of money–in the sixth century *or* the twentieth. The king's absurd discussion about farming is built upon Twain's literary comic pattern of "stringing incongruities together." Note that the Boss brings more money in the slave market than does the king–a source of humiliation to King Arthur.

CHAPTER 35

A PITIFUL INCIDENT

Up until this time, King Arthur has ignored all of the Boss's suggestions that slavery be abolished. Finally the king understands the value of the Yankee's comments. (Because of this triumph, the Boss does not really regret that they have become slaves.) During a severe storm one winter evening, the slave-driver begins to see his profits disappear for, one after another, the slaves are dying with the cold. All of a sudden, a woman runs up to the group of slaves, begging for protection. A mob of people pursuing her claims that she is a witch and should be burned. The slave master tells the mob that the girl will be given up—if they will burn her beside his slaves. With the body of the wretched girl furnishing fuel, there was soon a nice warm fire going. Then the slaves are driven on to London. A young girl, fondling a baby, has been accused of stealing. A priest tells the crowd that she has stolen only to feed her baby but that the law of the land has no choice but to demand her death. The priest tells the people that the young woman's husband "was waylaid and impressed, and sent to sea," and his young wife had no means of support. Just before the young girl dies, the priest promises to care for her baby.

CHAPTER 36

AN ENCOUNTER IN THE DARK

In the sixth century, London is a village of mud and thatch. Surveying the village, the Boss begins to make plans about escaping. One day, he removes a pin from the garment of a would-be purchaser. During the night, after the other slaves are asleep, the clever Yankee unlocks the padlock on his chains with the pin. Before the Boss can unlock the king's padlock, the slave master comes in to check his property and then departs. Since the plan is to overcome the slave master, the Yankee goes after him but accidentally attacks the wrong man. The authorities appear, and the Yankee and his opponent are marched to jail.

CHAPTER 37

AN AWFUL PREDICAMENT

After a sleepless night in jail, the Yankee is taken to a court, where he makes believe that he has been on an errand for a very important man. He claims that the other man engaged him in a fight. The Yankee is dismissed from the court, and hurries back to the slave quarters to find no one there. He searches the place carefully and finds the dead body of the slave master. A bystander relates how, during the previous night, the slaves revolted and killed the master. The authorities know that one of the slaves (the Yankee) has escaped. The law is such that, if one slave kills his master, the rest of that man's slaves must die for it. The Yankee is upset, for he knows that King Arthur is among the condemned slaves. The Boss makes his way to a small shop which has been converted to a telegraph office, and insists that the telegraph operator place a call to Camelot. Soon, Clarence is being given directions as to what he must do: five hundred knights are to be led by Sir Launcelot. The Boss then hurries away to second-hand clothing stores, to buy clothes suitable for the reception of Arthur's knights. Unfortunately he is again captured and sent to jail with the other slaves.

CHAPTER 38

SIR LAUNCELOT AND KNIGHTS TO THE RESCUE

The time for the slaves' execution has been moved forward one day. The Boss realizes that Launcelot and the five hundred knights will never get to London in time. When the king is freed of his bonds, preparatory to being hanged, he proclaims to the crowd that he is Arthur, King of Britain. They laugh at him. One by one, the slaves are hanged. Just as the king is blindfolded, the Yankee is thrilled to see racing toward him "five hundred mailed and belted knights on bicycles!" Arthur is quickly released and the crowd kneels, begging his forgiveness.

CHAPTER 39

THE YANKEE'S FIGHT WITH THE KNIGHTS

Back at Camelot, the Boss is pleased to read his morning paper at the breakfast table. The feature story is the announcement of a forthcoming tournament, featuring Sir Sagramor and himself. The Yankee knows that his opponent represents not only Merlin, but also all of King Arthur's knights. (The Boss has been encroaching on the knights' privileges.) At the tournament, Sir Sagramor rides forth, "an imposing tower of iron, stately and rigid." The Boss appears in "flesh-colored tights." Sir Sagramor places his lance in position and comes "thundering down the course" toward the Yankee. When the knight gets very near to the Yankee, the latter swerves aside, and the knight rides by. This maneuver is carried out sucessfully several times. Finally, the Yankee throws a lasso over the knight, and soon the tower of iron is being dragged along the ground. With the crowd cheering, one after another, the knights of the Round Table suffer the same fate. Then the Yankee's luck changes, for Merlin steals his lasso. Sir Sagramor again heads toward the Yankee. When the charging knight is fifteen paces away from the Boss, there is a loud explosion. The Boss has shot a revolver, and Sir Sagramor is dead. Furious, all of the knights ride toward the Yankee, but when eleven of their number are killed, they stop.

COMMENT (Chapters 35-39): Notice that the king, once in favor of slavery, is now opposed to it—since he has actually experienced the horrors of the institution. The British system of impressment of men into military service is criticized, as demonstrated in the horror of the young woman who is hanged. The Boss's plan for a showy and picturesque rescue of the king is reminiscent of Tom Sawyer's plan for rescuing Jim in *Huck Finn.* Notice that the shift ahead in time of the execution of the slaves (in Chapter 37) is similar with the setting ahead of the day of the Yankee's execution (in Chapter 6). What an unexpected twist there is in the story when Launcelot and his knights arrive on bicycles to rescue the king and the Boss! (One motion picture version of the story features motorcycles instead of bicycles.) The Boss is entering the lists (the tournament) to "destroy knight-errantry or be its victim." What a dramatic contrast there is between the two opponents—Sir Sagramor, "an imposing tower of iron "in his armor, and the Boss in the "flesh-colored tights" of his gym costume. (The lasso act must have been splendidly worked out in the motion picture, starring cowboy Will Rogers as the Boss.) Twain arranges the opposing forces in a dramatic tableau: all of the knights of the Round Table and Hank stand, "a hundred yards apart, facing each other, rigid and motionless, like horsed statues." The Boss wins.

CHAPTER 40

THREE YEARS LATER

The Boss has now achieved a great reputation. He no longer needs to work in secret. Three years pass by quickly. King Arthur's nation has changed; there is no more slavery, and all men are now equal before the law. Numerous labor-saving devices operate to make people happy. The Boss is entertaining an idea "to send out an expedition to discover America." King Arthur's knights still wander about the countryside—but with a new purpose. No longer are they hunting for the Holy Grail; they are attempting to persuade people to buy sewing machines on the installment plan, or perhaps to subscribe to a prohibition journal. If people do not succumb to their salesmanship, there is a brief scuffle, and the knights ride on. There is only one fly in the ointment, and that fly is the power of the estabilshed church. The Boss entertains an idea that after King Arthur's death England can become a republic—he secretly believes he might make a good president. The Boss has married Sandy, and the happy couple have a baby girl, named "Hello-Central." Suddenly, the baby becomes ill, but the Boss's nineteenth-century knowledge saves her. The doctors recommend taking the baby to the sea, and so the Boss and Sandy leave Camelot for a month.

CHAPTER 41

THE INTERDICT

Hello-Central begins to improve in health. For the first time in two and one-half weeks, the worried parents begin to think of other things. Suddenly, the Boss realizes that the ship he had sent back to Camelot had not returned, and anxiously goes back himself. In Canterbury he finds that the bell in the belfry is "shrouded in black . . . its tongue tied back." He realizes that the established church has struck with the Interdict (excommunication). All England seems still; even the electric lights have been snuffed out. The Boss approaches the castle at Camelot, which he enters unchallenged.

CHAPTER 42

WAR!

In his quarters, Clarence explains what has happened. For years, Queen Guenever has been looking longingly into the eyes of Sir Launcelot. Only one person in the kingdom has not noticed this, King Arthur. Because Sir Launcelot offended two nephews of the king, they tell Arthur about Guenever and Launcelot. Eventually war is declared, with the nation divided between the king's party and Sir Launcelot's. Many knights have been killed. Finally, Arthur himself dies, and Guenever retreats to a nunnery. The established church has taken command. The Boss thinks that all of the people of the kingdom will come to his aid. Clarence explains that they very well might have done so—"until the Interdict." Clarence has cleverly prepared for a seige—fifty-two boys (between the ages of fourteen and seventeen and not prone to superstition) have helped build an electrified fortification. Instead of going underground however, the Boss decides to take the offensive and proclaims a republic.

CHAPTER 43

THE BATTLE OF THE SAND-BELT

The Yankee has had electrical lines connected with the foundations of all the great factories. He sends word to the people in the factories to vacate immediately as he plans to explode all of the buildings. From all over England the knights gather—their goal, to blot out the Boss. When the advancing army is close to the fortification, there is a thunderous noise and all but a few are blown to bits. Clarence and the Yankee make a tour of the electrified fences. The remaining knights try another attack, riding into a deep ditch surrounding the fence, but a mountain brook is released into the ditch, creating a deep river. The last of the knights are drowned.

CHAPTER 44

A POSTSCRIPT BY CLARENCE

The story is concluded by Clarence. He and the Boss had made a tour of the battle ground. When the Boss tried to help a wounded man, the man stabbed him. The Boss was carried back to the camp, where an old woman appeared who volunteered to nurse him. Clarence later discovered the woman "making curious passes in the air" over the Boss's head. "She" is revealed as Merlin who boasts he has destroyed all the boys with his magic and they were dying—all except the Boss who is destined to sleep for thirteen centuries.

FINAL P.S. BY M.T.

The author, Mark Twain, has been reading the manuscript brought in by the stranger. In the morning, he goes to the room of the unusual man, who is in bed deleriously talking to someone named Sandy. He mutters that he has been dreaming he had been thirteen centuries into the future. He is very happy to have returned to his dear Sandy. Mistaking Twain's hand for Sandy's, the stranger holds it close to him. Then he dies.

COMMENT (Chapter 40-"Final P.S. by M.T."): Over a period of three years, the Boss has almost completely reorganized the English social and economic system. Note that both Hank and King Arthur are now about forty years old. The account of Clarence's idea about a "royal family of cats" (in Chapter 40) is amusing. The reader may be somewhat startled to find that the Boss has married Sandy. Clarence's account of the war between the forces of King Arthur and Launcelot (in Chapter 42) reads somewhat like the long mediaeval romances Sandy previously told on her adventure with the Boss, such as in Chapter 15, "Sandy's Tale." Note that Clarence has chosen "boys" (to protect the fortification) who are too young to have been very much effected by the superstitions of their elders. Near the beginning of Chapter 43, the Boss writes of turning his old diary into narrative form. (This narrative form, of course, is the manuscript supposedly being read by Mark Twain.) Notice the effectiveness of inserting two letters from the Boss into Chapter 43. The knights, electrified by the fence, resemble statues (in Chapter 43). Beginning with Chapter 44, the story is still told in the first person singular, but the "I" is now Clarence, who describes the wounding of the Boss and the fact that the Boss "sleeps like a stone." Clarence indicates that the "Manuscript" is to be hidden "with The Boss . . . be he alive or dead." In the "Final P.S. by M.T.," the stranger seems to be mentally returning to Sandy, as observed and reported by Mark Twain.

CHARACTER ANALYSES

HANK MORGAN: The Yankee is first seen as a "curious stranger" who attracts Mark Twain's attention because of his "candid simplicity, his marvelous familiarity with ancient armor and the restfulness of his company." His conversation is soft, pleasant and flowing but he speaks of strange things—"transposition of epochs . . . and bodies."

Hank is an American, "born and reared" in Hartford, Connecticut and a "practical" Yankee, . . . "nearly barren of sentiment." He does not panic when suddenly and inexplicably uprooted to a strange land, but sensibly proceeds to solve his problems in "their proper order." Yankee ingenuity comes to his rescue many times: he terrifies attacking knights by blowing smoke from his pipe through the bars of his helmet, playing upon their superstitious fear of dragons; a strategically placed electric fortification wins a battle in which he is greatly outnumbered; even the mighty Merlin has a difficult time competing with the Yankee's lifesaving feats of "magic."

The former head superintendent of a munitions plant is quite capable of using wiles based on his common-sensical knowledge of psychology to advance his cause. In the valley of Holiness, nineteenth-century know-how and a keen awareness of the people with whom he is dealing, combine to create a reputation-building "miracle." The Boss feels tournaments are "very stirring and picturesque . . . but just a little wearisome to the practical mind." However he attends them, for he considers his attendance politic. In chapter 37, Hank's complicated lie to the court is mindful of Huck Finn's guide. In the same chapter, his elaborate plan for rescuing the king is reminiscent of Tom Sawyer's rescue of Jim in *Huckleberry Finn*.

The Yankee views the French Revolution as a glorious thing and speaks of "loyalty . . . to one's country, not to its institutions or its office holders." He feels that most of the "free population" of the country is in a state of virtual slavery, and plans to establish a republican form of government in England after Arthur's death—he thinks of himself as a good candidate for president.

Hank refers to himself as a Presbyterian and feels religion should be left to an individual's choosing. He believes that "any Established Church is an established crime." He makes fun of "saints of the Roman calendar," and terms Benvenuto Cellini ("ten centuries later") a "rough-hewn saint." His "idea" about religion is "to have it cut up into forty free sects, so that they will police each other."

The Boss evaluates himself as "a man of knowledge, brains, pluck and enterprise"; his power is colossal—he is second in command to King Arthur. People come from great distances to view the Boss and he willingly displays himself "a dozen times a day . . . to . . . reverent and awe-stricken multitudes." He considers "the Boss" a respectful title, as unique and meaningful as "the King."

This powerful figure is not devoid of a sense of humor and frugality. He recollects his boyhood days when he always saved his "pennies and contributed buttons to the foreign missionary cause." He enjoys spending money on Marco's party, but is irritated when Dowley cannot understand the objective value of money. His sense of humor is evident in the signs carried by the roaming knights ("Persimmon's Soap—All the Prime-Donne Use It"). He can also be ironically humorous as when he advocates having "nobodies" as officers, "selected on a basis of mere efficiency."

Over a period of three years, the Boss has accomplished many things. He has brought the industrial revolution to medieaval England and has succeeded in eliminating the superstitions which have kept the people in fearful and apathetic bondage. He has even managed to marry the girl he loves and start a family.

KING ARTHUR: The king is an admixture of virtue, superstition and majestic gusto. His subjects refer to him as "Arthur, the king whose word is gold!" He is revered as a "wise and humane judge." He does his "honest best and fairest–according to his light."

Conflicting with these virtues are superstitions and primitive values. The Boss observes that the king's "rearing" colors his decisions. Arthur thinks in terms of a false hierarchy of classes –he only approves of those officer-candidates with aristocratic heritages. When Hank and the king are sold as slaves, Arthur is more concerned over the fact that the Yankee has brought a higher price than he has. The Boss is granted enormous power in Camelot simply because of the king's superstitious awe of the Yankee's "magical" prowess. Obviously thinking he is himself imbued with magical abilities, Arthur holds court on a "king's-evil day," at which his ailing subjects come forth to be granted money and cured by the touch of the king.

But Arthur struggles valiantly to overcome his defects. Hank and the king undertake an arduous journey to gain first-hand knowledge of the country's problems. The king goes to great lengths to appear as a commoner: the Boss cuts off the lustrous hair and drills him in speech and mannerisms. Unfortunately, Arthur's acting does not prove equal to his good intentions. At the conclusion of Marco's party, the king (masquerading as "Jones," a farmer) chats about agricultural life with enthusiaastic ignorance. Strange combinations of farm products, such as onions and berries, "plums and other like cereals" and the "juice of the . . . cabbage" start the uneasy villagers thinking they are dealing with a madman. When he begins to speak of the ripeness of a goat, they fall fearfully and murderously upon the king. Nevertheless, there are positive results from the difficult journey: Arthur learns to value his subjects qua human beings; he places his own health in jeopardy nursing smallpox victims. He observes the innocent victims of injustice and is greatly affected. At the end of the trip, he no longer sanctions slavery and institutes sweeping reforms throughout the nation.

The king has an enthusiasm for life which takes various forms. As a warrior he is "in raptures" over the opportunity for adventure—slaying fierce dragons, rescuing maids in distress or undertaking a hazardous journey to learn about his people. As a man he is kingly. His enormous pride in himself is difficult to disguise. The king's "style" is what discourages slave-buyers from purchasing him. He is described as a "two-dollar-and-a-half chump with a thirty-dollar style." During his enslavement Arthur maintains his grand spirit—even though his body is mutilated by "lash and club and fist."

BRIEF SUMMARY OF *THE MYSTERIOUS STRANGER*

In the winter of 1590, the small village of Eseldorf in Austria is filled with superstitious peasants still mentally living in the Middle Ages. Three young village boys, Nikolaus, Seppi and Theodor enjoy the freedom of the hills and valleys nearby. In Eseldorf, are two priests–Father Adolf, who is respected because he insists that he has "no fear of the Devil" and Father Peter, who is beloved by the villagers, but discredited by Father Adolf. (Father Peter is said to believe that God is "all goodness" and will save "all" of his children. Father Adolf maintains that this is impossible.) A more powerful enemy was the astrologer also opposes the gentle Father Peter. Everyone in the village except Father Peter stood in awe of him. The villagers feared the astrologer because of the magical powers he claimed to possess but the brave priest openly denounced him as a charleton.

A youth of their own years who declares that he is the nephew of "Satan" appears before the three boys. His earthly name is Philip Traum, but he is known to the boys as "Satan." Throughout the story, Satan performs numerous "miracles" to amuse them. He builds a castle filled with small quarreling men and women only to destroy it, because he is impatient with the stupidity of men in general–and with these newly created individuals, in particular. He is unimpressed with man, for he is "made of dirt," is a "museum of diseases" and has "the Moral Sense." To test man's virtue, Satan fills Father Peter's lost wallet with money. When the wallet is found, the priest is accused of stealing the money from the astrologer. In court, Satan saves Father Peter by revealing that all of the money was minted *after* the date when the wicked astrologer claims to have possessed it.

Satan then takes his three small friends all over the world to witness how unkind man can be to man. The young visitor alters the arrangement of events in certain people's lives. Theodor is told that Nikolaus will die within twelve days to spare him endless years of suffering, for it is appointed that he live out the rest of his life as a wretched paralytic. Seppi and Theodor are in mental agony, for they recollect all of the mean things that they have done to their doomed friend. Nikolaus is drowned in an attempt to save the life of a small child. After a year of occasional visits, Satan stays away from Eseldorf for "a long time." He returns for a final visit and informs Theodor that "Life itself is only a vision, a dream" and that he (Satan) is a "dream," the "creature" of Theodor's "imagination." Theodor is told that in the future, he should "Dream other dreams, and better ones."

DETAILED SUMMARY OF *THE MYSTERIOUS STRANGER*

1.

The time is 1590. The place is the sleepy little village of Eseldorf, Austria. The villagers are devout churchmen, revering "the Virgin, the Church, and the saints above everything." Knowledge is not considered "good for the common people." There are two priests. Father Adolf is widely respected, for he claims to have "actually met Satan face to face more than once, and defied him." Father Peter is loved by the people, for he is "always good and gentle and truthful." He is said to believe that God will save "all his poor human children." Father Peter denounces the malevolent astrologer who is believed to have magical powers. The bishop has suspended Father Peter, so he and Marget (his niece) now live in poverty.

2.

Three boys roam the "hills and woods" near the village. They are Nikolaus Bauman, Seppi Wohlmeyer, and Theodor Fischer (the story-teller). Sometimes the boys visit with Felix Brandt, an old servant in the castle on the hill who tells them stories about ghosts and angels. One May morning, a strange youth strolls toward the boys in the woods. He has fine clothes and a pleasing manner. He performs an astonishing feat of magic by lighting a pipe merely by blowing on it. Then he performs a variety of wonderous tricks: he causes water to become ice; he fills the boys' pockets with different kinds of fruits; out of clay, he makes both a squirrel and a dog, both of which seem to be living. He claims to be an angel named "Satan" (nephew to the better known "Satan"). While he talks, he makes five hundred little men and women ("the size of your finger"), who begin to build a little castle. Theodor wants to ask if Satan has seen his uncle and, reading his mind, Satan answers

"Millions of times." As Satan crushes two of the little workmen who are quarreling, he says that he "cannot do wrong," for he does "not know what it is." Suddenly, he tires of the noises made by the newly-created little people, and he mashes many of them into the earth with a heavy board. But the "music of his voice" enchants the three boys into forgetting the horror of his deed, so "drunk [were they] with the joy of being with him."

3.

Satan has seen all, been everywhere, knows everything and forgets nothing. As he talks of the great men of the earth, his "manner" reveals that "to him they and their doings" are "of paltry poor consequence." He matter-of-factly mentions that men are "dull and ignorant and trivial and conceited, and . . . diseased and rickety, and . . . a shabby, poor, worthless lot all around." Soon, a bad thunder storm sets the little castle on fire, and all of the five hundred newly-made people are killed. Satan says: "they were of no value." A little later he says that he goes by the name "Philip Traum." He tells the boys that he will "protect" (quiet) their tongues, so that they will not be able to speak of the deeds he has performed. Father Peter comes along the path and walks "straight through Satan," proving the visitor's statement that he (Satan) is "only a spirit." Satan lists three things he finds typical of man: "Man is made of dirt . . . Man is a museum of diseases . . . And man has the *Moral Sense*." Soon, Satan leaves the boys—gradually dissolving himself away. Father Peter returns to find his wallet, stuffed with money (put there by Satan). The boys encourage him to use the over "eleven hundred ducats" to pay the mortgage on his house.

4.

The next day when Father Peter pays the mortgage and has a great deal of money left over, "cool old friends" become "kind and friendly again." Theodor asks Father Peter to define the "Moral Sense." The priest replies: "it is the faculty which enables us to distinguish good from evil." Now that the family is accepted again, Marget's (Father Peter's niece) deserted pupils return for their spinnet lessons. Her admirer, Wilhelm Meidling who remained faithful waits for her.

5.

The astrologer appears on the fourth day, and claims that Father Peter has stolen the money from *him*. When the three boys tell of watching Father Peter finding the wallet with the money, the villagers are angry with them and insist that the boys are telling a lie. Father Peter is put in prison. Four days later Marget's servant, old Ursula, appears at Theodor's house and asks for some work so she can buy food for herself and the starving Marget. On her way home afterwards, Ursula sits beside the road and pets a "lean stray kitten in her lap." Satan appears and senses the old woman's goodness. He calls the kitten a "Lucky Cat," for every morning its owner will find "four silver groschen in his pocket." Suddenly Ursula finds four coins in her own pocket and gratefully blesses her benefactor. Theodor wishes he might see Marget, and Satan whisks the two boys to Marget's parlor. Marget is there and wanly greets them. During the conversation, Satan mentions his uncle, who is "in business down in the tropics" and who is "very well off" because of his "monopoly." Satan gives Marget a paper (on which he has scribbled some marks) which will admit her to see her uncle in prison. (Theodor knows the "marks" are an "enchantment.") Satan so maneuvers the conversation that Marget has to invite the two boys to supper. Miraculously, all kinds of good foods appear on the table. (Marget is amazed, but she accepts her good fortune. Ursula thinks Agnes, the cat, is responsible for the feast. Theodor knows that Satan has provided everything.) After dinner, Marget goes to see her uncle, and Satan takes Theodor on a visit to a "torture-chamber." Theodor is upset at the totrture being administered to a suspected "heretic," and he calls the torture "a brutal thing." Satan says: "it was a human thing . . . No brute ever does a cruel thing—that is the monopoly of those with the Moral Sense."

6.

Satan takes Theodor to a great factory in a French village, where "worn and half starved" people are working. Satan observes they have committed no crimes to cause them to be subjected to such daily misery; they are in this condition solely for having been born into the human race. Back in the village again, the two boys meet Seppi, who tells of the disappearance of Hans Oppert, "the village loafer," who badly mistreats his dog. Satan comments that Hans's actions are "quite distinctly human." The dog appears, and Satan talks with it and learns that Hans has fallen over a precipice. In Father Peter's house Marget is again in reasonably good spirits. There is now money enough–so much money, in fact, that Ursula has hired another servant, Gottfried Narr (whose grandmother was "burned as a witch"). Theodor remembers eleven school girls who were "put on bread and water for ten days and ten nights" before they confessed to being witches. They were burned at the stake. Gottfried begins to be popular with people who wonder what is happening in Father Peter's house and the silly young boy brags of the quantities of food and money they have. Father Adolf instructs the villagers to spy on Marget, for he believes witchcraft is at the bottom of the new prosperity.

7.

Marget invites forty people to a party to be held seven days later. During this week the house is constantly watched. No food enters it from outside and yet, when Father Adolf arrives, fine food is seen everywhere. Satan arrives and is much admired by the other guests. The astrologer (without invitation) joins the party and (by accident) notices that the bottle of wine, which he is served from, always stays full. Father Adolf declares the house "bewitched and accursed" and the guests hurriedly leave. The people are frightened at the thought that "witches and devils" have visited their village. They fear that word will reach the outside world and that the "Interdict" (excommunication) will be declared against them. Only Wilhelm refuses to desert Marget. Satan tries to charm her depression away somewhat to Wilhelm's jealous displeasure.

In the middle of the night, Satan decides to take Theodor on a journey to China. The Austrian boy tries to "reform" Satan. Satan is amused and explains the power of his mind. He is able to create in reality anything he may conceive. Since what man calls his mind is nothing but chaos, he, with his superb intellect, is infinitely superior–the difference cannot even be compared. Satan cannot really love even the good men he has found but he is fond of them and aids them when he can. He goes on to explain that man's circumstances and environment set his life into a pattern. If one link in this chain of events is disturbed, the whole pattern will change. Then Satan tells Theodor that Nikolaus's chain of events is to be changed and in twelve days, Nikolaus is to die. He is sparing Nikolaus forty-six years of agonizing paralysis. He also claims that Father Peter will be happy for "the rest of his life."

8.

Theodor begins to remember the times when he has not treated Nikolaus well. He tells Seppi the news and the grief-stricken boys begin to spend much of their time with Nikolaus. On the day designated for their friend's death, they visit him at his house. His mother instructs him to look for little Lisa who seems to be lost. In a few minutes, the drowned bodies of both Nikolaus and Lisa are brought to the house. Lisa's mother speaks out against God, and Fischer (the weaver) reports her to the authorities. She is to "go to the stake." Satan produces a "history of the progress of the human race," mostly featuring wars and conflicts.

9.

Satan often takes the two boys (Theodor and Seppi) with him on tours of the world. A woman is hunted down as a witch. Theodor throws a stone at her (even though he likes her), for he is afraid *not* to throw a stone at her. Satan tells Theodor that, of the sixty-eight people in the mob, only six had a desire to harm the woman. Satan says that the human race "is made up of sheep. It is governed by minorities, seldom or never by majorities."

10.

Satan has not visited Eseldorf for some days now. Marget asks her jealous admirer (Wilhelm Meidling) to defend her uncle at the trial. The astrologer, in the witness box, tells his story, accusing the priest of stealing from him. The two boys tell their tale, and the people laugh at them. Suddenly, Theodor realizes that Satan is melting into the body of Wilhelm. The "reactivated" lawyer now begins to address brilliant questions to the astrologer. Father Peter's good name is cleared when the court investigates the dates on the coins. The coins were almost all minted *after* the time when the astrologer claims he first possessed them. Satan hurries to Father Peter and tells him: "The trial is over, and you stand forever disgraced as a thief–by verdict of the court!" Father Peter loses his reason and becomes "as happy as a bird"–he thinks he is "Emperor." Satan tells Theodor that Father Peter "will remain . . . the one utterly happy person in this empire." Satan and Theodor travel to India, where they watch a juggler perform his tricks. Satan reacts to the cruelty of a "foreigner" by punishing him.

11.

Satan visits Eseldorf, off and on, for about a year. One day, he returns to say farewell to Theodor "for the last time." He says: "we shall not see each other any more." When Theodor asks if they will meet in another life, Satan says: "There is no other." He continues, "Life itself is only a vision, a dream. . . . I am but a dream–your dream, creature of your imagination." Then Satan disappears, leaving Theodor alone, believing Satan's words to be true.

COMMENT: Popular, glossy, and quick analyses of *The Mysterious Stranger* endlessly repeat each other. The inevitable comments are that, as Twain grew older, family sickness and death caused him to become depressed. They support this with Satan's parting thrust–man should dream other and better dreams. The striking contrast is almost always drawn between Twain the humorist (of the early years) and Twain the pessimist (of the later years).

Mark Twain's lack of skill as a self-critic is commonly known (as illustrated by the esteem he had for one of his minor works–*Personal Recollections of Joan of Arc*). However, in the case of *The Mysterious Stranger,* he may have been quite correct when (in a letter, dated 1906) he commented that this work was not finished. A. B. Paine (an important Twain biographer) has been lauded for selecting from among the Twain papers an appropriate earlier ending for *The Mysterious Stranger*. Possibly the selected ending is suitable, but the reader is abruptly jarred from what seems to be the middle of the tale to a hurried conclusion (typical of the "all-must-be-answered-endings" of romantic novels of the period). The meaning of the final "dream" section has been debated, as well it should be. Twain writes best in episodes (picaresque style), perhaps best evidenced by *Huckleberry Finn. The Mysterious Stranger* is highly episodic, with each segment representing another facet of the main thesis that man is far removed from the province of the angels.

Twain writes this book in what W. L. Phelps so aptly called "Indignation." In almost white-hot anger, he documents his belief in man's stupidity, his blindness and his everlasting selfishness. Twain's evidence mounts in episode after episode, as he argues his case. He begins his argument as if he were analyzing the seven deadly sins. Beginning with "pride," he offers the boastful Father Adolf. Using a familiar Twain literary technique, pride is followed with its opposite (or antithesis), Father Peter's belief that God is "goodness" and will save all of His "children." In turn, Twain demonstrates envy, anger, covetousness and gluttony in the manipulations of Father Adolf and the astrologer. (Anger and gluttony are given lighter treatment than the other two.) To follow this pattern satisfactorily, Twain needs episodes to support the concepts of lust and sloth. Being basically of a prudish nature and surrounded by the high fences of late-nineteenth-century Victorianism, he has difficulty in producing an episode on "sex." (Twain certainly may be considered a realist, but never a naturalist, for he almost ignores sex in his works.) Then, too, he has trouble representing the "sin" of sloth (laziness), for he has often presented the relaxed life as an attractive one, —Huck Finn's lazy drifting and Colonel Seller's charming indolence.

Since Twain's arguments are not all offered, it is possible to think of the work as delightful (because of its thought-provoking qualities), but incomplete (because the ending appears problematic. However, Twain's use of the "dream" fits splendidly into his pattern. Dreams are highly episodic and they sometimes ramble on from one place to another, with apparently little meaning or connection sequences. In *The Mysterious Stranger,* Satan suddenly arrives and just as suddenly whisks his youthful admirers to distant parts of the globe—France, China or India. There are no links necessary, for "It is all a dream—a grotesque and foolish dream."

Satan refers to a fixed chain of events in one's life. Using a literary context, this could refer to the Aristotelian cause and effect method of storytelling, with each succeeding chapter is based upon the previous one. In contrast to this literary technique, Twain generally depicts his heroes' adventures in episodes of the picaresque style. This technique most perfectly utilizes Twain's own individualized, spontaneous and optimistic style. He emanates assurance that there will continue to be endless episodes—that life will continue to plunge merrily onward without ceasing. Since he sees *no end* of episodes, since there is always tomorrow, Twain has difficulty in satisfactorily ending most of his works. (Even *Huckleberry Finn* has annoyed readers and critics alike with its problematic conclusion.) It is not in Twain's nature to end a literary work—at least, to end it in accordance with the standards of most writers. His long fictional and non-fictional works remind one of a long distance runner who, at the end of a difficult race, limply drops to the ground. There is no pep or spirit left for the grand display—the big smile and waves for the camera. This is true of the tacked-on ending of *The Mysterious Stranger* and the conclusion of the long, uneven autobiographical work *Life on the Mississippi,* with the last paragraph quickly shuttling Twain and the reader back to the East.

The Austrian village, Eseldorf (meaning "town of jackasses"), is rather like Hannibal, Missouri, Twain's boyhood home town, seen as St. Petersburg in *Tom Sawyer* and *Huck Finn.* There is the same nostalgic picture of woods and river. One of Theodor's comments on the weather could come from *Huck Finn:* "I fell asleep to pleasant music that night—the patter of rain upon the panes and the dull growling of distant thunder" (section 7).

The three boys are reminiscent of Tom and Huck and the members of "Tom Sawyer's Gang." The astrologer is pictured like one of St. Petersburg's "town characters." Although there are pleasant memories of Hannibal throughout *The Mysterious Stranger,* also present is a cloud of gloom, of pessimism, of disillusion and of disenchantment. There is the lack of trust in the constants (the eternal truths) of life. "Friends" come and go at Marget's house, according to how much money she has. Wicked characters such as Father Adolf and the astrologer often succeed in their schemes. Twain's satire on the benefits of the Church has a sharp edge, unlike the almost melodramatic, satirical picture of the "Established Church" in *A Connecticut Yankee in King Arthur's Court.*

Father Adolf's hunger for power is vividly pictured. He imagines that his pronouncement of the existence of "witchcraft" at Father Peter's home, will carry his name with it, and make him renowned forever . . . the glory of it" makes him "dizzy." Twain cynically pictures religion as inspiring fear, rather than love, in a power "struggle for existence." He pessimistically contends that thought or acts independent of the mob will be rewarded with death (such as the stoning and hanging of the lady who cared for sick people, in section 9). "Satan" is a curious admixture of good and evil. He is used almost as if Twain was not sure he had the ability to portray the extent of his cynicism and pessimism; thus, he introduces a *deus ex machina* character who can manipulate the events of people's lives, to help prove Twain's thesis concerning the moral blindness and mental stupidity of man.

Of interest, might be a few more brief references to Twain's literary technique in *The Mysterious Stranger,* as well as parallels to other Twain works. The title word "Stranger" is an adaptation of the "unknown" character of the Gothic romance of horror and terror. The paragraph (in section 3) describing the final ruin of the miniature castle is quite reminiscent of the concluding paragraph of Poe's tale, "The Fall of the House of Usher." The miscounting of the coins (in section 5) is similar to another incident, involving the counting of spoons in Huck Finn. In section 7, reference is made to "the Interdict"; near the end of *A Connecticut Yankee in King Arthur's Court,* the "Interdict" fells King Arthur's kingdom. Satan and Theodor sit on a mountain top and survey the surrounding area (in section 7), much like characters in Cooper's *Leatherstocking Tales* climb to heights and look about them. Twain emphasizes the "tranquil" and "dreamy" aspects of the nature description, whereas Cooper often inserts a moral overtone into his nature pictures. One is reminded of the "duality of man" (in section 7) when Satan says: "Every man is a suffering-machine and a happiness-machine combined." Also in the same section is a strong parallel to Robert Frost's poem "The Road Not Taken" in the paragraph beginning with "Forear-doin it? No." In Section 8 Theodor is describing the eleven days, immediately before the death of Nikolaus. He indicates that "with a lifetime stretching back between to-day and then, they are still a grateful memory to me." (Suddenly, the reader is aware that Twain is using a flash-back technique.) In section 8 is an example of human cruelty (the carpenter's disposal of Lisa's Brandt's corpse). Satan says that this is standard behavior for "members of the human race," but he adds that horses would not act "in such a way." One remember's Twain's admiration for Jonathan Swift's *Gullivers Travels,* Part 4 of which describes horses as being morally superior to men. During Mark Twain's early successful days as a humorist on the lecture platform, he based much of his appeal on broad, frontier, Western humor. Near the end of *The Mysterious Stranger,* in section 10, the reader is startled to find Twain ridiculing his early audiences and his own, special brand of humorous stories. Satan says that the human "race" has a "mongrel perception of humor," for it sees "the comic side of a thousand low-grade and trivial things—broad incongruities, mainly; grotesqueries, absurdities, evokers of the horse-laugh."

CHARACTER ANALYSIS

SATAN: Satan's earthly name is Philip Traum—"Traum" is German for "dream." He is first pictured as a handsome stranger dressed in "new and good clothes," with a "winning face and a pleasant voice." He is "easy and graceful and unembarrassed," and "not slouchy and awkward and diffident, like other boys." Being "earnest and simple and gentle," he talks "alluringly" "in his soft, persuasive way" to the boys. He performs miracles, such as producing a variety of fruit (out of season) and creating living animals out of clay. He says he is "sixteen thousand years old" and the "second favorite" of his well-known uncle. He claims to be an "angel," "ignorant of sin," incapable of committing it. He adds that he is "without blemish" and shall remain "in that state always." As he crushes two quarreling, tiny people between his fingers and wipes the blood from his fingers, he ironically refers to all of the angels: "We cannot do wrong." The "fatal music of his voice" makes the boys "drunk with the joy of being with him." Satan has "seen everything," "been everywhere," knows "everything," and forgets "nothing." He feels that "men and women here on the earth and their doings" are of "paltry poor consequence." He says that human beings are "quite interesting to him," but they are "dull and ignorant and trivial and conceited, and . . . deseased and rickety, and . . . a shabby, poor, worthless lot all around." He is "full of bubbling spirits" but mentions men as one might speak of "bricks." He, himself, is an "immortal." Marget considers him "beautiful." He is kind to her and her maid, Ursula. After Father Adolf has declared Marget's home "betwitched and accursed," she is unhappy—until Satan comes in, "fresh and cheery and beautiful," and charms her into a pleasant mood. Wherever he goes he is like a "fresh breeze to the weak and the sick." To Satan, "time and distance" have no limits. What could be "weeks and months" to man might be "a fraction of a second" to him, an immortal. He so fascinates the boys that village life seems "dull without him" nearby. At the end of the story, Satan says that he has "no existence"—that he is "a dream," the "creature" of Theodor's "imagination." In the last line of the tale, he vanishes.

BRIEF SUMMARY OF
LIFE ON THE MISSISSIPPI

Mark Twain begins this autobiographical account of his Mississippi River experiences by briefly discussing the physical statistics and the early explorers of the river. He includes a fictional account of activities on a river raft. His own early desire to be a river pilot leads him to become an apprentice-pilot under Mr. Horace Bixby. He suffers much humiliation, but he finally becomes a full-fledged pilot. He remembers the river at high water time and recalls the "soundings" for depth, when the river is low. He learns to cultivate the keen observation of details all of which he must remember. He pictures the operation of the river pilots' association, and thinks of the days when steamboats raced each other on the river. The story of the *Pennsylvania* steamboat fire is filled with colorful details.

(Beginning with Chapter 21, the account of river life is told from the viewpoint of Mark Twain, who returns to the Mississippi twenty-one years after finishing his piloting days.) He notices changes in clothing styles along the river; there are fewer steamboats than before. He meets old friends and revisits scenes of his youth. Cities, such as Memphis, (Tennessee) have changed after several decades. He uses stories and legends such as "The Professor's Yarn," heard near Vicksburg, Mississippi. Manufacturing in beautiful Natchez and the Sir Walter Scott Capitol building in Baton Rouge both seem to irritate Twain. The sights of New Orleans (from its above-ground cemeteries to its pictures of Generals Jackson and Lee) all become the butt of Twain's light-hearted satire. Sports and dances are described, as are the Mardi Gras and Sir Walter Scott's influence on Southern ideas.

The two-thousand mile trip by steamboat from New Orleans to St. Paul (Minnesota) carries Twain by the river cities of

St. Louis, Marion City, and Keokuk. He spends three days in his own home town, Hannibal, Missouri. At La Crosse, Wisconsin, an old gentleman entertains the passengers with Indian legends and travel talks. After noting the high points of both St. Paul and Minneapolis, Mark Twain hurries East to New York City by way of Chicago.

DETAILED SUMMARY OF *LIFE ON THE MISSISSIPPI*

The first twenty of these sixty chapters are expressions of Mark Twain's boyhood admiration for the activities centered around the Mississippi River. The physical dimensions of the river and its early explorers are described. A story about Huck Finn and a river raft is inset in one chapter. (This portion did *not* later become a part of *The Adventures of Huckleberry Finn.*) All of the boys in Twain's home town (Hannibal, Missouri) enjoy and admire the workers on the river boats. The young Twain leaves home, all the time planning to realize his dream–to become a pilot. Finally, Mr. Horace Bixby agrees to teach the aspiring pilot. Twain learns, as a part of his new work, to observe carefully all of his river surroundings. He learns how to adapt his piloting to the times when there is high water; he learns how to take "soundings" (for the depth of the water) when the river is low. He finds that a pilot needs to do more than just *observe* his surroundings. He must also *remember* them. Twain learns of the pilots' organization (a union) to protect their interests. Sometimes, the steamboats race on the Mississippi River. Once in a while, the river changes its course and becomes shorter in total length. Twain tells of an infamous character, named Stephen, who borrows a great deal of money from all of his friends, never having an intention of repaying them. The apprentice-pilot Twain has much difficulty serving under a pilot named Brown. There is a vivid description of a fire aboard the *Pennsylvania,* following the explosion of four boilers.

Beginning with Chapter 21, Twain sketches his activities during the twenty-one years since he was a Mississippi River pilot. About 1882, he revisits the scenes of his piloting activities. He notices a great variety of clothing and hairdressing styles in different regions of the country. Both the towboat and the railroad have assumed much of the transportation of goods, once mainly assigned to the steamboats. Twain travels incognito, without allowing people on the river to know of his experiences there. His identity is discovered by a pilot whom he recognizes; and then he happily takes over the wheel of that pilot's boat for awhile. There is talk of the "Mississippi war-fleet" during the Civil War, as well as feuding among some of the people who live near the river. Twain records the reactions of numerous former travelers on the Mississippi. He pictures Memphis, Tennessee, as well as Helena, Arkansas. He recalls a "Dying Man's Confession" he once heard in Munich, Germany. He learns that Napoleon, a town he once much admired, has been washed away by the Arkansas River. A Vicksburg couple tell him what life was like during the shelling of the city during the Civil War. There is a short story about gambling at cards, told him by a college professor. Three months after leaving the boat, the *Gold Dust,* he learns that many people have recently been killed and severely injured on that vessel.

Twain describes the interior furnishings of a typical home of socially prominent people who lived near the river. He also pictures a "big fine steamboat," in its new and elaborately decorated state. He writes of Natchez, Mississippi–not as a great social center, but as a manufacturing town. Baton Rouge is described, as is the state of Louisiana, architecturally inspired by Sir Walter Scott. The geography of New Orleans is explored. Twain describes the cemeteries with their "vaults . . . above the ground." Features of the city are emphasized, such as the old iron railings and traditional pictures of Generals Jackson and Lee. The cock-fight and the mule-race are depicted. The "Mardi-Gras festivities" and the destructive influence of Sir Walter Scott on the South are both described in detail. Twain greets Joel Chandler Harris ("Uncle Remus") when he arrives from Atlanta. George Washington Cable's "next-to-impossible French names" are discussed. Twain is pleased to meet his former piloting instructor, Horace Bixby. A trip to a sugar plantation is described. Twain pokes fun at the questions asked at a *séance.* Most of Mark Twain's former pilot friends retire from the river to become farmers. Notes from the diary of Captain Isaiah Sellers are quoted in detail. Captain Sellers used to submit "brief paragraphs . . . about the river, and sign them 'Mark Twain,' and give them to the New Orleans Picayune (newspaper)." After Sellers' death, Samuel Langhorne Clemens adopts the old riverman's pseudonym.

Twain leaves new Orleans, headed for St. Louis, on the boat, the *City of Baton Rouge,* under Captain Horace Bixby's command. There are memories of a stage-struck youth, who for years had the walk-on part of a Roman soldier in Shakespeare's plays. The career of a fake letter, supposedly written to a man in prison, is analyzed in detail. On a visit to his home town (Hannibal, Missouri), Twain is told of the success of some of his village companions. Hannibal has changed into a commercial center. Twain remembers the circumstances surrounding the death of Lem Hackett who drowned on a Sunday. The village "Model Boy" is recollected and (again) disliked. The story of "Jimmy Finn, the town drunkard," who was burned to death in the town jail is related. North of St. Louis, Quincy and Marion City are seen from the steamboat. The career of Henry Clay Dean (of Keokuk, Iowa) is traced out, in detail. Burlington, an "Upper River" town, is discussed, as is Muscatine. Twain travels the river past Davenport, Dubuque, and Prairie du Chien. At La Crosse (Wisconsin), an "old gentleman" tells Indian legends and gives detailed travel talks, all based upon his experiences as a lecturer with a panorama. (See "Comment.") At St. Paul, "the head of navigation of the Mississippi," Twain finishes his two-thousand-mile voyage from New Orleans. Both St. Paul and Minneapolis are written up. "A Legend of White-Bear Lake" (a tale connected with a nearby lake) is inserted here. Traveling by train, Twain quickly hurries through Chicago and concludes his five-thousand-mile journey in New York City.

COMMENT (Chapters 1-20): As the reader excitedly prances through the first twenty chapters of *Life on the Mississippi,* he must not forget the literary term "dramatic propriety." (This term means that every word or thought coming from a character's mouth does not necessarily represent truth or the author's own point of view. Each word or thought may only represent what a character *might* possibly think under certain dramatic circumstances. An author's dialogue is generally intended to interest a reader rather than give him a picture of truth.) In the first chapters of *Life on the Mississippi,* Mark Twain draws a romantically, highly-colored picture of his early Mississippi River days, using a style rather like a long dramatic monologue, with Twain as the leading character. The river is his foil—that is, the river is used to illustrate how *he* feels about life, and to point out (either humorously or satirically) the varieties of prejudices and stupidities as common among men in the Mississippi River Valley as elsewhere. Just as many mediocre plays have succeeded because of brilliant direction, so has this highly individualized account of the Mississippi River come to life because of *its* "director," Twain. With the passage of time, most memories take on a rosy tinge—what might at one time have seemed "rotten," at a distant time might seem "mellow."

The first twenty chapters, entitled "Old Times on the Mississippi," were written for the *Atlantic Monthly,* and published serially in 1875. (Three of the original titles Twain offered for his series of articles help one realize the scope of the first chapters: "Steamboating on the Mississippi in Old Times," "Personal Old Times on the Mississippi," and "Piloting on the Mississippi in Old Times." The title finally chosen for the series was "Old Times on the Mississippi.") With himself as the leading character, Twain proceeds to romanticize his early ardent desire to become a pilot. He dramatizes his apprenticeships under Horace Bixby and Brown by the inclusion of many details. He uses a familiar Twain technique, verisimilitude (likeness to truth), causing the reader to feel that there must be truth in the stories—why else should there be so very many specific details as to exact times and places. Twain uses the appeal of many successful biographies, as he forges his way from "cub-pilot to pilot"—"from rags to riches." The descriptions of the Mississippi River, by night and by day, are interspersed among exciting and comic anecdotes of steamboating before the Civil War. Most of the "rough and tumble" activities, common on the Mississippi (as recorded in works by John Habermehl and George Deval), are eliminated from Twain's romantic picture. In the late nineteenth century, the *Atlantic Monthly* did not cater to scenes of immorality.

Twain, the leading character of the first chapters of his

book, has been compared to Huck Finn, who also followed the river and who was initiated into some of the mysteries of life, both good and bad. In *Life,* the focus is carefully set on one aspect of river existence–piloting. Note the familiar Twain technique of inserting entire units of extraneous material into the middle of the discourse. For example, in Chapter 3 ("Frescos from the Past"), most of the chapter is devoted to an episode in the life of Huck Finn, as he becomes involved with the activities on a huge river raft. Twain claimed that he incorporated this episode into his work to help illustrate "keelboat talk and manners . . . and raft life." The language of the river characters Twain cited is pure and spotless. In Chapter 5, a mate is said to be "sublime in the matter of profanity." Yet, when Twain quoted his vigorous dialogue, the worst of his profanity came out as "Dash it to dash!" One wonders if the last paragraph of Chapter 5 (concerning the "humbug" who "absorbed wildcat literature and appropriated its marvels") might not be an autobiographical reference. The dialogue in Chapters 8, 9, and 10, between Mr. Bixby and young Twain, suggests the minstrel-show patter between two end men. In Chapter 11 ("The River Rises"), the description of poor families, living on flatboats at high-water time, recalls Twain's descriptions of sixth-century, poverty-stricken families in *A Connecticut Yankee in King Arthur's Court*.

Chapter 13 ("A Pilot's Needs) offers a splendid discussion of three qualities needed by a good pilot: "a memory," "good and quick judgment and decision" and "calm, cool courage." Chapter 15 ("The Pilots' Monopoly") could well be included in the history of trade unions. The pilots were proud of an "organization . . . formed for the protection of their guild." "Racing Days" (Chapter 16) could be a fine essay in itself, independent of the book. Twain was very proud of his understanding of the dramatic monologue in which one character speaks to a silent listener. (He professed to be an expert interpreter of the famous dramatic monologues written by Robert Browning.) The Chapter 17 monologue by Stephen might well be used as a separate dramatic reading. The cub-pilot's mistreatment at the hands of Brown (in Chapters 18 and 19) helps stimulate the reader's sympathy for one who might be considered somewhat arrogant. Chapter 20 ("A Catastrophe") dramatically closes the first of the two parts of *Life on the Mississippi.* Although Mark Twain was not "on the spot" during the fire on the river steamer, the *Pennsylvania,* his account (filled with vivid journalistic detail) allows one to see the mounting flames and hear the shrieks and groans.

COMMENT (Chapters 21-60): In a letter, dated August 30, 1906 (published in *Mark Twain in Eruption,* edited by Bernard DeVoto), Twain explains his theory that an unfinished work may be put aside for a time—perhaps a few years. After a proper interval, the book may be taken up and finished without difficulty. For examples, he refers to the interruptions in the middle of both *The Prince and the Pauper* and *A Connecticut Yankee in King Arthur's Court.* What was evidently true for these stories was *not* true for the completed *Life on the Mississippi.* The time interval was eight years, between 1875 (the date of publication of the *Atlantic Monthly* articles) and 1883 (the date of the completed work), incorporating forty more chapters). Whereas the first sketches were dredged up (out of Twain's romantic memories of his experiences as a river pilot), the latter essays were stimulated by an actual journey of five thousand miles which the writer took, revisiting his youthful haunts and refreshing his memory. Part one featured Twain as the main character, as he dramatically "used" the river and all of its activities to help further a picture of his own education as a river pilot. The mood is romantic and nostalgic. In part two (Chapters 21 through 60), Twain assumed second place in the literary scheme of things, as he became the biographer (or recorder, or gazetteer) of the Mississippi River. Much of the romantic sparkle and glitter of Chapters 1 through 20 have disappeared. As far as most of the last two-thirds of the volume is concerned, a reader could learn about as much of the Mississippi River from atlases or travelogues. Very little distinguishes one chapter from another—except the reasonably interesting chapter headings. Chapter 21 is the transition chapter between the two parts of the book. Beginning with Chapter 22, Twain relates his revisit to the river which he left twenty-one years before. He sees the area with the eyes of a tourist—a tourist viewing the scenes of his early struggles. Chapter 27 ("Some Imported Articles") records impressions of the river, taken from "tourist-books" of past travelers, such as Captain Basil Hall (in 1827), Mrs. Trollope (in 1827), the Hon. Charles Augustus Murray (in 1834) and of Captain Marryat (in 1837). Then Twain continues by quoting Alexander Mackay, Captain Basil Hall (again), and Francis Parkman. One interesting character emerges—Uncle Mumford. (Note especially Chapters 25 and 28.) Chapter 29 ("A Few Specimen Bricks") includes two effective pictures of Memphis, Tennessee—one by a German tourist and one by Mrs. Trollope.

In Chapter 31, Twain inserted a story ("A Dying Man's Confession"), told in the first person singular—his favorite device for storytelling. Chapter 33 ("Refreshments and Ethics") offers a fine variety in literary pace with the inclusion of a barkeeper's quotation. "Vicksburg During the Trouble" (Chapter 35) is a very interesting account of the siege of Vicksburg, told by the natives of the city. Again using the first person singular, Twain relates a story told by a fellow passenger, a college professor (Chapter 36). One of the most brilliant chapters of the entire book is Chapter 38 ("The House Beautiful"), a detailed picture of a Southern mansion, comparable to the Grangerford's home in *Huck Finn*. Natchez, Mississippi (once the social center for the western part of the old South) is pictured as a manufacturing town in Chapter 39.

Chapter 40 ("Castles and Culture") begins, and Chapter 46 ("Enchantments and Enchanters") continues Mark Twain's vehement protest against what he considered the evil influence of Sir Walter Scott on the South. Chapters 41 through 50 describe Twain in New Orleans. He pokes fun at New Orleans' cemetery vaults above ground (Chapter 42); he visits the historical highlights (Chapter 44); he discusses cock fights, mule races, and women

(Chapter 45); he greets two literary friends–Joel Chandler Harris ("Uncle Remus") and George Washington Cable (Chapter 47).

Chapter 49 ("Episodes in Pilot Life") has moments comparable to some fine episodes in the first twenty chapters. When Twain starts to discuss piloting, the content sparkles a bit more than ordinarily. Chapter 50 offers Twain's explanation of how he happened to assume the penname "Mark Twain." Chapters 53 through 56 are concerned with Twain's visit to his home town, Hannibal, Missouri. The reader hopes in vain that, at long last, Twain might become a rhapsodic, in contrast with most of the prosaic pace of the rest of the last chapters of *Life on the Mississippi.* Nothing changes. Twain used more feeling in his descriptions of New Orleans than he did of Hannibal. (The end paragraph of Chapter 54 is an exception; here is described "the Model Boy" of Hannibal–which the famous Tom Sawyer was *not.*) The story of a spontaneous orator, Henry Clay Dean of Keokuk, is told in an entertaining manner. (Twain once worked in Keokuk, Iowa in a print shop.) Chapter 58 reads like a travel brochure describing suitable towns to visit.

In Chapter 59 ("Legends and Scenery"), Twain varies his travel account by making believe he is listening to an "old gentleman" lecture on the glories of the river towns. The old man also tells an Indian legend. Twain thinks the "old gentleman" might once have lectured using a "panorama." Popular lectures in the nineteenth century, were organized around a series of pictures representing a continuous scene, arranged to unroll and pass before the spectator (like a typewriter ribbon). One of the most popular lectures, using the "panorama," was of a trip on the Mississippi River. The last chapter, 60 ("Speculations and Conclusions"), is amazingly dull, with its statistics about St. Paul and Minneapolis–how much school teachers were paid yearly in the former, and how many pupils and teachers there were in the latter. A long story, which Twain called an "idiotic Indian legend," is included in the chapter. After reading a few general comments about the legend, the reader finds himself—with no preparation—reading the *last* paragraph of a long book. In moments, the journey is over. There are four appendices to the work. Appendix A concerns three excerpts from the New Orleans *Times-Democrat* describing flood conditions, one entitled "Voyage of the 'Times-Democrat's' Relief-Boat Through the Inundated Regions," one labeled "Down Black River," and another called "The Flood Still Rising." Appendix B is a letter signed "Edward Atkinson," concerned with flood control of the Mississippi River. Appendix C is a reviewer's comments on the "Reception of Captain Basil Hall's Book in the United States." Appendix D is "The Undying Head," an Indian legend, mentioned at the end of Chapter 59.

CRITICAL COMMENTARY

A Connecticut Yankee in King Arthur's Court, Life on the Mississippi, and *The Mysterious Stranger* are among Mark Twain's most widely read and discussed books. Any major criticism of Twain's works must have reference to these three works. The following brief summary of criticism is subdivided into three parts: (1) Mark Twain biography, letters and bibliography; (2) collected works and specialized editions; and, (3) critical commentary of Mark Twain and his works.

(1) **MARK TWAIN BIOGRAPHY, LETTERS AND BIBLIOGRAPHY:** There are numerous biographies of Twain, some of the most important of which are listed chronologically as follows. Twain, himself, provides much of the material for the study in three volumes by A. B. Paine, entitled *Mark Twain, A Biography* (1912). This early, affirmative picture of Twain is for the general reader—not the scholar. In 1920, Van Wyck Brooks's *The Ordeal of Mark Twain* tries to prove that Twain is thwarted in his literary development, not only by his Missouri background, but also by his later Victorian and wealthy friends in the East. Bernard DeVoto in *Mark Twain's America* (1932) attacks the Brooks thesis and claims that Twain's development was greatly enhanced by his frontier background. Edward Wagenknecht, in *Mark Twain: The Man and His Work* (1935, 1961), argues for the view that Twain's works reflect his frontier background and his own attitudes toward life. In 1943, DeLancey Ferguson, in *Mark Twain: Man and Legend,* stresses the environmental and literary influences which helped to develop Twain into a prominent literary figure. Dixon Wecter's *Sam Clemens of Hannibal* (1952) emphasizes the part played in Twain's development by his hometown, Hannibal, Missouri. Kenneth Andrew's 1950 book, *Nook Farm: Mark Twain's Hart-*

ford Circle, pictures the influences of the East on Twain, who (late in life) yearns for the simplicity of his early, Mississippi River Valley days. A relatively late work which helps broaden one's view of Twain the person is Caroline T. Harnsberger's *Mark Twain: Family Man* (1960). Jerry Allen's *The Adventures of Mark Twain* (1954) is a very readable biography. Frank Baldanza's *Mark Twain: An Introduction and Interpretation* (1961) offers a good introductory picture of the most celebrated authors of the Mississippi River Valley.

Mark Twain's letters throw interesting light on him as a person and as a developing literary artist. Among the collections of letters available is A. B. Paine's two-volume edition of *Letters, Arranged with Comment* (1917), as well as Dixon Wecter's two editions, *Mark Twain to Mrs. Fairbanks* (1949) and *The Love Letters of Mark Twain* (1949). Some other sources of letters are: Ivan Benson's *Mark Twain: Business Man* (1946); G. E. Dane's edition of *Letters from the Sandwich Islands* (1937, 1938); Thomas Nickerson's collection, *Letters from Honolulu* (1939); Cyril Clemens' *Republican Letters* (1941); E. M. Branch's edition, *Letters in the Muscatine Journal* (1942); E. E. Leisy's collection, *The Letters of Quintus Curtius Snodgrass* (1946); Theodore Hornberger's edition, *Mark Twain's Letters to Will Bowen* (1941); and "Mark Twain's Letters in the San Francisco *Call*" (*Twainian,* 1949, 1952).

Mark Twain bibliography is found in numerous places. Of primary importance is Merle Johnson's *A Bibliography of the Works of Mark Twain, Samuel Langhorne Clemens* (1935). Of value is the alphabetical listing in Lewis Leary's *Articles on American Literature, 1900-1950* (1954). A splendidly workable edition of references to Mark Twain is Harry Hayden Clark's "Mark Twain," in *Eight American Authors,* ed., Floyd Stovall (1956). (Consult the 1963 "Bibliographical Supplement" by J. Chesley Mathews for additional references.)

(2) **COLLECTED WORKS AND SPECIALIZED EDITIONS:** Four collected editions are available: *The Writings of Mark Twain,* edited by A. B. Paine, 37 volumes (1922-1925); the Author's National Edition of *The Writings of Mark Twain,* 25 volumes (1901-1907); and *Mark Twain's Works,* 23 volumes (1933).

Many of Twain's letters and speeches are included in collections of periodicals. (See Lewis Leary's *Articles on American Literature, 1900-1950,* as well as Harry Hayden Clark's "Mark Twain," *Eight American Authors.*) Charles Neider has published a number of the short Mark Twain selections in several volumes. Special collections of Mark Twain manuscripts may be found in the following places: The Berg Collection of the New York Public Library; the William Dean Howells Papers at Harvard; the Boston Public Library; the Huntington Library; the Princeton Library; and the Library of Congress. (H. N. Smith, of the University of California, has in his charge numerous unpublished manuscripts, the property of the Mark Twain estate.)

(3) **CRITICAL COMMENTARY ON MARK TWAIN AND HIS WORKS:** Much has been written on Twain, both the man and the works. First, consider influences and sources. In 1937, Walter Blair places Twain within the general tradition of *Native American Humor.* See, also, Constance Rourke's *American Humor,* 1931, concerning the elements of folklore in Twain's works, R. W. Frantz's "The Role of Folklore in *Huckleberry Finn,*" *American Literature* (1956), and R. E. Bell's "How Mark Twain Comments on Society through Use of Folklore," *Mark Twain Quarterly* (1955). Earlier, in 1934, Minnie M. Brashear wrote of the part Twain's Hannibal (Missouri) background played in his literary development, as well as the influence of eighteenth-century writers, such as Swift and Thomas Paine (*Mark Twain: Son of Missouri*), to his progress. G. A. Cardwell's *Twins of Genius* (1953) contains the thirty-eight letters exchanged between Mark Twain and his influential literary friend, George Washington Cable. See, also the following two thoughtful articles: P. J. Carter's "The Influence of the Nevada Frontier on Mark Twain," *Western Humanities Review* (1959) and Henry Nash Smith's "Mark Twain's Images of Hannibal: From St. Petersburg to Eseldorf," University of Texas *Studies in English* (1958).

Much of Twain's work is concerned with the question of man's ethical conduct. To some extent, Gladys C. Bellamy discusses this aspect of Mark Twain in her book, *Mark Twain As a Literary Artist* (1950). Three articles review some portions of Twain's ethical attitudes: H. H. Waggoner's "Science in the Thought of Mark Twain," *American Literature* (1937); R. T. Oliver's "Mark Twain and Religion," *Christian Leader* (1940); and, F. C. Flowers's "Mark Twain's Theories of Morality," *Mark Twain Quarterly* (1948). See, also, the two following studies: G. M. Rubenstein's "The Moral Structure of *Huckleberry Finn*," *College English* (1956) and A. E. Jones's "Mark Twain and the Determinism of *What Is Man?*" *American Literature* (1957).

Readers of *The Prince and the Pauper* and *A Connecticut Yankee in King Arthur's Court* are keenly aware of Mark Twain's strong political and social points of view. V. L. Parrington's *Main Currents in American Thought* (Volume III) (1930) underlines Twain's attack on monarchy and the established church. See, also, A. L. Scott's "Mark Twain Looks at Europe," *South Atlantic Quarterly* (1953). Concerning the Civil War and Twain, at least three articles have been written: John Gerber's "Mark Twain's 'Private Campaign,'" *Civil War History* (1955); F. W. Lorch's "Mark Twain and the 'Campaign that Failed,'" *American Literature* (1941); and G. H. Orians's "Walter Scott, Mark Twain, and the Civil War," *South Atlantic Quarterly* (1941). Some other studies emphasizing Mark Twain's political and social aspects, are Paul Carter's "The Influence of W. D. Howells upon Mark Twain's Social Satire," University of Colorado *Studies* (1953); A. L. Scott's "Mark Twain: Critic of Conquest," *Dalhousie Review* (1955); F. R. Leavis's "The Americanness of American Literature," *Commentary* (1952); and, Earl Hilton's "Mark Twain's Theory of History," *Papers of the Michigan Academy of Science, Art, and Letters* (1951, 1952). Two relatively recent books and two articles should be of interest to the reader of Mark Twain with an interest in his political-social activities: P. S. Foner's *Mark Twain: Social Critic* (1958); R. B. Solomon's *Twain and the Image of History* (1961); P. J. Carter's "Mark Twain and the American Labor Movement," *New England Quarterly* (1957); and, Sherwood Cummings's "Mark Twain's Social Darwinism," *Huntington Library Quarterly* (1957).

Mark Twain's ideas on literary composition and his aesthetics philosophy are scattered throughout the works. Once in a while, Twain wrote essays on literature as such–for example "How to Tell a Story" and "Is Shakespeare Dead?" Besides Gladys C. Bellamy's excellent book, *Mark Twain as a Literary Artist* (1950), and the index to the comprehensive *Transitions in American Literary History,* ed., Harry Hayden Clark (1953), there are other aids toward understanding Twain's individualized approach to fiction. Some of the outstanding articles are: Brander Matthews's "Mark Twain and the Art of Writing," *Harper's* (1920); S. E. Liljegren's "The Revolt Against Romanticism in American Literature as Evidenced in the Work of S. L. Clemens," *Studia Neophilologica* (1945); G. W. Feinstein's "Mark Twain's Idea of Story Structure," *American Literature* (1946); E. H. Goold's "Mark Twain on the Writing of Fiction," *American Literature* (1954); R. A. Wiggins's "Mark Twain and the Drama," *American Literature* (1953); Harry Hayden Clark's "The Influence of Science on American Literary Criticism, 1860-1910, Including the Vogue of Taine," *Transactions of the Wisconsin Academy of Sciences, Arts, and Letters* (1955); Pascal Covici's *Mark Twain's Humor: The Image of a World* (1962); F. R. Roger's *Mark Twain's Burlesque Patterns: As Seen in the Novels and Narratives 1855-1885* (1960); H. N. Smith's *Mark Twain: The Development of a Writer* (1962); Sherwood Cummings's "Science and Mark Twain's Theory of Fiction," *Philological Quarterly* (1958); Otto Friedrich's "Mark Twain and the Nature of Humor," *Discourse* (1959); J. C. Gerber's "The Relation between Point of View and Style in the Works of Mark Twain," in *Style in Prose Fiction: English Institute Essays* (1958), ed., H. C. Martin; J. B. Hoben's "Mark Twain: On the Writer's Use of Language," *American Scholar* (1956); and S. J. Krause's "Twain's Method and Theory of Composition," *Modern Philology* (1959).

Numerous studies of Twain's language have been made, some of the most important being: F. G. Emberson's "Mark Twain's Vocabulary: A General Survey," University of Missouri *Studies* (1935); R. L. Ramsay and F. G. Emberson's "A Mark Twain Lexicon," "University of Missouri *Studies* (1938); Katherine Buxbaum's "Mark Twain and American Dialect," *American Speech* (1927); C. J. Lowell's "The Background of Mark Twain's Vocabulary," *American Speech* (1947); and, H. L. Mencken's monumental *American Language* (1930).

Among the histories of American fiction, which deal with Mark Twain, five might be mentioned: A. H. Quinn's *American Fiction* (1936); W. F. Taylor's *A History of American Letters* (1936); Carl Van Doren's *The American Novel: 1789-1939* (1940); Alexander Cowie's *The Rise of the American Novel* (1948); and Edward Wagenknecht's *Cavalcade of the American Novel* (1952). Prominent among the histories of American literature are three works which discuss Twain: *The Cambridge History of American Literature* (essay by S. P. Sherman) (1921); V. L. Parrington's *Main Currents in American Thought* (Volume 3) (1930); and, *A Literary History of the United States* (essay by Dixon Wecter) (1948).

For comprehensive annotations concerning studies of *Huckleberry Finn* (currently, Twain's most popular book), see Harry Hayden Clark's "Mark Twain," *Eight American Authors* (1963 edition), pp. 347-355. For a discussion of other individual works of Mark Twain, see, also, H. H. Clark's section on Twain in *Eight American Authors,* pp. 355-361. For those who find of interest Frank Luther Mott's comments on Mark Twain in *Golden Multitudes: The Story of Best Sellers in the United States* (1947), reference might be made to Roger Asselinean's *The Literary Reputation of Mark Twain from 1910 to 1950: A Critical Essay and a Bibliography* (1954).

Two helpful collections of essays about Mark Twain and his works are: Henry Nash Smith, ed., *Mark Twain: A Collection of Critical Essays* (Twentieth Century Views Series) and Guy A. Cardwell, ed., *Discussions of Mark Twain* (*Discussions of Literature* Series) (1963). Lewis Leary's *Mark Twain* (University of Minnesota Pamphlets on American Writers) (1960) is a good, general introduction. (See, also, Lewis Leary's edition, *A Casebook on Mark Twain's Wound,* (1962.) E. H. Long's *Mark Twain Handbook* (1958) is worthwhile for broad coverage of Twain material.

ESSAY QUESTIONS AND ANSWERS

1. What did Mark Twain think of his fellow men?

ANSWER: Mark Twain was very disappointed in his fellow men. In his *Biography,* he wonders why the human race was created and considers it a pity that Noah and his party did not miss the boat. Twain considered that man was base, hypocritical, and cruel. Often ready to praise achievement, he nevertheless observed that the majority of men were not innovators but simply followed the handful that made the most noise. Whether this handful was most times wrong or right in their leadership was a secondary issue; what was relevant was the sheep-like tendencies of the crowd. Twain criticized, belittled, and scolded, but owned that man had one stupendous superiority—his intellect and imagination—by virtue of which he could reach heights. Hank in *A Connecticut Yankee,* a simple New Englander, was able to remake an entire country using his ingenuity. Twain also admired energy, ambition, productivity and certain other virtues. He was almost convinced that it was possible for man to reach heroic stature (see *Personal Recollections of Joan of Arc*), but was not really sure what he expected that stature to consist of. That is, Twain admired certain men, but only for what he himself lacked. He was certain that there really was no objective standard and maintained that we consider heroic only those men who do things we cannot do.

Evidently troubled, Twain felt that there was a moral code, but man did not and, most probably, could not adhere to it. For instance, he was almost awe-struck when he spoke of truth, but held that only the dead were permitted to speak it. He considered truth to be one of those virtues required by the best in man, but the practise of it just too impractical for man's daily living. Twain discussed morals in his *Biography,* stating that the ". . . morals of the Lord have been . . . the morals of the first-created man; . . . but the morals of mankind are the morals of necessity . . . the morals of mankind have kept pace with necessity, whereas those of the Lord have remained unchanged.

2. What was Mark Twain's attitude toward the church?

ANSWER: Mark Twain had no respect for the established church, although he professed a belief in God. He considered that the church had opposed every innovation and discovery throughout history. He was, for instance, incensed at the church censure of the use of anesthetics at childbirth on the ground that it avoided the biblical curse pronounced against Eve. An individualist, Twain fervently adhered to the concept of freedom of worship. In *A Connecticut Yankee,* Hank, in speaking of the religious institutions he has set up, says: "I could have made everybody a Presbyterian without any trouble, but that would have been to affront a law of human nature . . . man is only at his best morally . . . when following that religion best suited to his individual preference."

Twain contended that centuries of horror and torture had been perpetrated because no religion was really great enough or divine enough to be tolerant of other religions. He maintained that the established church was nothing more than a political machine antipathetic to human liberty.

Twain was really no more enamoured of God than with the church. He believed in the existence of a supernatural being primarily to explain the nature of the universe. He considered that a consciousness had created and was maintaining the universe. But in thinking of a personal God, Twain was most dissatisfied. He called the God of the Bible "an irascible, vindictive, fierce and ever fickle and changeful master. . . ." In constructing the kind of God he would like, Twain imagined a dignified diety, unboasting, unassuming and, above all, taking upon Himself the responsibility of sin and relieving man of this burden.

3. List and discuss Mark Twain's pessimistic view of man, as projected through the mouth of Satan in *The Mysterious Stranger*.

ANSWER: Satan tells the boys (in section 3) that man is "dull and ignorant and trivial and conceited, and . . . diseased and rickety, and . . . a shabby, poor, worthless lot all around." The "angel" says that "Man is made of dirt," that he is "a museum of diseases," and that he has the *"Moral Sense."* (Father Peter later defines "Moral Sense" as "the one thing which lifts man above the beasts that perish and make him heir to immortality.") Satan is amused that man is supposed to be able " to distinguish between right and wrong"–and that "in nine out of ten cases, he prefers the wrong"–all the time considering himself superior to animals who do "not inflict pain for the pleasure of inflicting it" (section 5). Satan continues, saying that man is "such an unreasoning creature that he is not able to perceive that the Moral Sense degrades him to the bottom layer of animated beings." He points out that the toiling factory workers in the French village have committed no "crime." All they have done is to get themselves "born" into the "foolish" human "race." Satan declares man an "illogical, unreasoning race," and he laughingly pokes fun at man's "pride" in "warlike deeds . . . great heroes . . . imperishable fames . . . mighty kings . . . ancient aristocracies . . . venerable history." Satan looks at the three boys and (seeing them as representative of all men) says: "how few are your days, how childish your pomps, and what shadows you are!" When Seppi calls Hans Oppert, the village loafer, a "heartless brute," because he mistreats his dog, Satan retorts: "Brutes do not act like that, but only men." He says the "human race" was "not made of clay," but "it was made of mud–part of it was, anyway." When eleven young girls are murdered for witchcraft, Satan says that an animal "wouldn't drive children mad with hunger and fright and loneliness, and then burn them for confessing to things invented for them which had never happened." He muses that "Every man is a suffering-machine and a happiness-machine combined. . . . Sometimes for an hour's happiness a man's machinery makes him pay years of misery." He adds that "Man's mind clumsily and tediously and laboriously patches little trivialities together and gets a result–such as it is." Men "never know good fortune from ill," says Satan. To Theodor, he says: "You are a curious lot—your race." In section 8, he contends that "to kill" is "the chiefest ambition of the human race" and that "all the competent killers are Christians" and declares that "For a million years the race has gone on . . . monotonously reperforming this dull nonsense—war." He says that the human "race" is "made up of sheep" and that "It is governed by minorities, seldom or never by majorities." One of the few pleasant things Satan says about "man" is that "The vast majority of the race . . . are secretly kind-hearted and shrink from inflicting pain." Then he thoughtfully adds: "in the presence of the aggressive and pitiless minority they don't dare to assert themselves." To Theodor, Satan makes a sweeping generalization: "Monarchies, aristocracies, and religions are all based upon that large defect in your race—the individual's distrust of his neighbor, and his desire, for safety's or comfort's sake, to stand well in his neighbor's eye." (Note the "keeping-up-with-the-Joneses" overtones!) Later in section 10, Satan maintains that "No sane man can be happy, for to him life is real, and he sees what a fearful thing it is. Only the mad can be happy, and not many of those." Satan says that the "multitude see the comic side of a thousand low-grade and trivial things." (He recommends "laughter" as a means of removing human "juvenilities," for "Against the assault of laughter nothing can stand.") In section 11, Satan tells Theodor that *"there is no other"* life. He claims that *"life itself is only a vision, a dream"; "nothing exists save empty space"*—and the individual. Man's "universe and its contents" are "only dreams, visions, fiction!" He concludes by declaring that "man" is "but a *thought*—a vagrant thought, a useless thought, a homeless thought."

4. Mark Twain inserts many extraneous bits of material into *Life on the Mississippi,* his account of Mississippi River life. Discuss them and the reasons he offers for their being included.

ANSWER: In Chapter 2 ("The River and Its Explorers"), he quotes Francis Parkman's authentic historical description of the explorations of not only Marquette and Joliet, but also of La Salle. Chapter 3 ("Frescos From the Past") is mainly an episode in the life of Huck Finn. This fictional account was included "by way of illustrating keelboat talk and manners, and that now departed and hardly remembered raft life," writes Twain in 1875. In Chapter 16 ("Racing Days"), there are nearly three pages of statistics cited, under the headings: "The Record of Some Famous Trips" and "Fast Times on the Western Waters." Also, there is cited a "time-table from part to part" of the famous race in 1870 between the *R. E. Lee* and the *Natchez*. In Chapter 26 ("Under Fire"), one of the pilots on Twain's boat tells of "his first war experience in the Belmost fight, as a pilot on a boat in the Confederate service" (during the Civil War). The account, told in the first person singular, is entitled "The Pilot's First Battle." In Chapter 27 ("Some Imparted Articles"), Twain pokes fun at the "emotions produced in . . . foreign breasts by . . . aspects" of the river. He quotes from the travel journals of Captain Basil Hall, Mrs. Trollope, the Hon. Charles Augustus Murray, Captain Marryat, Alexander Mackay, and Francis Parkman. In Chapter 28 ("Uncle Mumford Unloads"), Twain consults the mate of his vessel about River Commissions and engineers. Twain quotes "the result, stenographically reported, and therefore to be relied on as being full and correct." The insertion (which is one long dramatic monologue) is called "Uncle Mumford's Impressions." At the end of the same chapter (28), Twain cites a paragraph from the Cincinnati *Commercial,* which describes the money saved by transporting coal by river rather than by train.

In Chapter 29 ("A Few Specimen Bricks"), Twain cites four pages of description of the famous "Murel's Gang"—"a colossal combination of robbers, horse-thieves, negro-stealers, and counterfeiters, engaged in business along the river some fifty or sixty years ago." The same chapter (29) concludes with two descriptions of the city of Memphis. The first "picture" is "drawn by a German tourist who seems to have been an eye-witness of the scenes" which he describes "in chapter vii of his book, just published in Leipzig." The other description of Memphis is by Mrs. Trollope. In Chapter 31 ("A Thumb Print and What Came of It"), Twain recalls a story told him when he "spent a few months in Munich, Bavaria" during the previous year. The long story is entitled "A Dying Man's Confession." The dying man, Ritter, wants Mark Twain to get some money, secreted in a "brick livery stable" in Napoleon, to send to a certain man. When Twain prepares to leave the boat at Napoleon (described in the next chapter, 32), he is informed that, years before, the Arkansas River washed away Napoleon into the Mississippi River, and that the whole town has disappeared. (Probably, these two chapters illustrate Twain's command of the tall tale, a favorite type of frontier humorous story.) In Chapter 35 ("Vicksburg During the Trouble"), Twain cites the account of the siege of Vicksburg, as seen by a man (a non-combatant) who lived through it, day by day. At the end of this chapter (35), Mark Twain introduces a story which becomes all of Chapter 36 ("The Professor's Yarn"), except for a brief concluding paragraph. Twain writes that he inserts this story "in this place merely because it is a good story, not because it belongs here—for it doesn't." The story is told by a "passenger—a college professor—and is called to the surface in the course of a general conversation," which ranges over topics such as horses, astronomy, dreams and superstitions. ("The Professor's Yarn" is about card gambling on a river boat.) Chapter 37 ("The End of the Gold Dust") cites a newspaper account of "A Terrible Disaster," wherein there are "Seventeen Persons Killed by an Explosion on the Steamer *Gold Dust*." In Chapter 39 ("Manufactures and Miscreants"), Twain quotes Mrs. Trollope's 1827 favorable comment on the charms of Natchez, Mississippi, as a stark contrast with the manufacturing aspects of the same town in 1882.

In Chapter 40 ("Castles and Culture"), Twain satirically places two sets of contrasting quotations in striking juxtaposition. One set of quotations, in the body of the chapter, presents first a "remark" from a "Female Institute" in Tennessee about the "beautiful architecture" of the "Institute building." This is followed by an "extract" from the "prospectus" (a printed advertisement) of a "Female College" in Kentucky. This "extract" places much emphasis on the South: "Believing the Southern to be the highest type of civilization this continent has seen, the young ladies are trained according to the Southern ideas of delicacy, refinement, womanhood, religion, and propriety." In contrast to these two extravagant pictures of Southern "civilization," Twain (in a long footnote) offers the case of a "feud" ending in the public killing of three men in the street (taken from an *Associated Press Telegram*). This is followed by three instances of brutal killings, generally by professional and "highly connected" people (cited from the *"Public Journals"*). Then, in an unflurried manner, Twain quotes both Mrs. Trollope and Captain Basil Hall—the former concerning the beauty of the Southern landscape, and the latter on the attractiveness of the houses and the "thriving air" of the "river scenery" on the Lower Mississippi. In Chapter 42 ("Hygiene and Sentiment"), Twain discusses the burial practices of the natives of New Orleans. He quotes the *North American Review* from an article about germs spreading from dead bodies in cemeteries to people living in the area. Twain follows this quotation with a long statement made by Dr. Charles W. Purdy in "an address before the Chicago Medical Society in advocacy of cremation." In Chapter 45 ("Southern Sports"), Twain argues that the "trouble with the Southern reporter" is "Women," for they "unsettle him . . . throw him off his balance." Twain says that the reporter becomes "flowery and idiotic," as evidenced by an elaborate description of women at a mule-race. (In contrast to this "flowery" description is a straightforward account of weather conditions, which does not mention women.)

In Chapter 50 ("The 'Original Jacobs' "), Twain quotes from the "diary" of Captain Isaiah Sellers, as reported in the St. Louis *Republican*. The excerpts represent general interest items, such as the timing of runs on the Mississippi River, as well as autobiographical references to Captain Seller's own career on the river. (Captain Sellers signed his "brief paragraphs of plain, practical information about the river" with the pen name "Mark Twain" and they were published in the New Orleans *Picayune*. Later, Samuel Langhorne Clemens permanently borrowed Captain Seller's pen name, at about the time of the old man's death.) In Chapter 52 ("A Burning Brand"), Twain quotes extensively from several letters about a "burglar named Williams . . . serving a nine-year term in a certain state prison." There is the original "faked" letter and several letters arguing for or against its authenticity. (The final evidence proves that the original "letter" was a "pure swindle," an effort "to get Mr. Williams pardoned out of prison.") In Chapter 59 ("Legends and Scenery"), Twain has "Schoolcraft's book" about Indian legends recommended to him by "an old gentleman." Twain quotes one of them (in Chapter 59): "Peboan and Seegwun, an Allegory of the Seasons"; in Appendix D, Twain reproduces another "long tale" of Indians, "The Undying Head." Near the end of Chapter 60, ("Speculations and Conclusions"), Twain cites the whole of "a most idiotic Indian legend, "connected with White-bear Lake (near St. Paul and Minneapolis). It is called "A Legend of White-bear Lake." (For a summary of the four appendices, see the last part of the "Detailed Summary of *Life on the Mississippi.*"

SUBJECT BIBLIOGRAPHY AND GUIDE TO RESEARCH PAPERS

The research paper should be based on careful reading of the texts of the original works which may be found in numerous editions, including paperback. Six paperback editions of *A Connecticut Yankee in King Arthur's Court* are brought out by the following publishers: Associated Booksellers ("Airmont"); Chandler Publishing Company; Harper and Row, Publishers, Inc.; Hill and Wang, Inc. ("American Century Series"); New American Library of World Literature, Inc. ("Signet"); and, Washington Square Press, Inc. Five paperback editions of *Life on the Mississippi* are available from the following publishers: Associated Booksellers ("Airmont"); Bantam Books, Inc.; Harper and Row, Publishers, Inc.; Hill and Wang ("American Century Series"); and, New American Library of World Literature, Inc. ("Signet"). Three paperbacks contain *The Mysterious Stranger: "The Mysterious Stranger" and Other Stories,* published by New American Library of World Literature, Inc. ("Signet"); *The Portable Mark Twain,* published by The Viking Press, Inc. ("Viking Paperbound Portables"); and, *The Complete Short Stories of Mark Twain,* published by Bantam Books, Inc.

There has been a great deal of criticism written about Mark Twain and his works. The following selective items include the most important criticism, with emphasis on *A Connecticut Yankee in King Arthur's Court, Life on the Mississippi,* and *The Mysterious Stranger*. The bibliographical listings have been arranged alphabetically by author for each research topic:

GENERAL: STANDARD CRITICISM AND INTERPRETATION

Questions to consider: Has critical opinion altered since the original publication of these works? Consider the main targets of Twain's satire, such as his attacks on the established church and Sir Walter Scott. How is Twain's own personality revealed in these works? In what ways do these books differ from the writing of other authors of the same period?

Baldanza, Frank, *Mark Twain: An Introduction and Interpretation* (1961).

Boynton, Percy H., "Mark Twain," *Literature and American Life* (1936).

Brashear, Minnie M., *Mark Twain: Son of Missouri* (1934).

Brooks, Van Wyck, *The Ordeal of Mark Twain* (1920, 1933).

Calverton, V. F., *The Liberation of American Literature* (1932).

Canby, Henry Seidel, "Mark Twain," *Definitions* (Second Series) (1924).

Cardwell, Guy A., ed., *Discussions of Mark Twain* ("Discussions of Literature" series) (1963).

Chase, Richard, *The American Novel and Its Tradition* (1957).

Clark, Harry Hayden, "Mark Twain," *Eight American Authors: A Review of Research and Criticism,* ed., Floyd Stovall (1956, 1963).

_______, ed., *Transitions in American Literary History* (1953).

Clemens, Samuel Langhorne, *Mark Twain's Speeches* (Introduction by Albert Bigelow Paine) (1910).

_______, *The Complete Essays of Mark Twain,* ed., Charles Neider (1963).

_______, *The Complete Humorous Sketches and Tales of Mark Twain,* ed., Charles Neider (1961).

_______, *The Complete Short Stories of Mark Twain,* ed., Charles Neider (1957).

Compton, C. H., "Who Reads Mark Twain?" *Who Reads What?* (1934).

Cowie, A., "Mark Twain," *The Rise of the American Novel* (1948).

DeVoto, B. A., "Introduction," *Portable Mark Twain* (1946).

_______, "Introduction to Mark Twain," *Literature in America*, ed., P. Rahv (1957).

_______, *Mark Twain's America* (1932).

Ferguson, DeLancey, *Mark Twain: Man and Legend* (1943).

Fiedler, L. A., *Love and Death in the American Novel* (1960).

Foner, Philip S., *Mark Twain: Social Critic* (1958).

Gerould, G. H., "Explorers of Varying Scenes," *Patterns of English and American Fiction* (1942).

Hicks, Granville, "Mark Twain," *The Great Tradition* (1933).

Howard, Leon, *Literature and the American Tradition* (1960).

Johnson, Merle, *A Bibliography of the Works of Mark Twain, Samuel Langhorne Clemens . . . .* (1935).

Knight, Grant C., "Mark Twain," *American Literature and Culture* (1932).

_______, *The Critical Period in American Literature* (1951).

Leary, Lewis, *Articles on American Literature, 1900-1950* (1954).

_______, *Mark Twain* (University of Minnesota, Pamphlets on American Writers) (1960).

Lewisohn, Ludwig, *Expression in America* (1932).

Long, E. Hudson, *Mark Twain Handbook* (1958).

Morley, C. D., "Hunting Mark's Remainders," *Streamlines* (1936).

Paine, A. B., *Mark Twain, A Biography* (3 volumes) (1912).

Parrington, Vernon Louis, "The Backwash of the Frontier—Mark Twain," *Main Currents in American Thought* (Volume 3) (1930).

Quinn, Arthur Hobson, *American Fiction: An Historical and Critical Survey* (1936).

Rubin, L. D., Jr., and J. R. Moore, eds., *The Idea of an American Novel* (1961).

Scott, Arthur L., *Mark Twain: Selected Criticism* (1955).

Smith, Henry Nash, *Mark Twain: A Collection of Critical Essays* (1963).

Snell, G. D., "Mark Twain," *Shapers of American Fiction, 1798-1947* (1947).

Spiller, R. E., "Literary Rediscovery: Howells, Mark Twain," in *Cycle of American Literature,* ed., R. E. Spiller (1955).
Spiller, Robert E., and others, eds., *A Literary History of the United States* (1955).
Stovall, F., "Decline of Idealism," *American Idealism* (1943).
Taylor, W. F., *A History of American Letters* (1936).
_______, "Mark Twain," *The Economic Novel in America* (1942).
Van Doren, C. C. "Mark Twain," *The American Novel: 1789-1939* (1940).
Wagenknecht, E. C., "Lincoln of Our Literature," *Cavalcade of the American Novel* (1952).
_______, Mark Twain: *The Man and His Work* (1935).
Wecter, Dixon, *Sam Clemens of Hannibal* (1952).

A CONNECTICUT YANKEE IN KING ARTHUR'S COURT ANALYZED

Question to consider: In what ways does Twain make a satirical attack on the established church. Discuss Twain's attack on feudalism. Consider the points of view of the several storytellers who relate the story. Note the varieties of literary techniques used in this romance. Is there evidence that Twain is interested in "clothes philosophy"?

Baetzhold, H. G., "The Course of Composition of *A Connecticut Yankee*: A Reinterpretation," *American Literature* (1961).

Blair, Walter, *Horse Sense in American Humor* (1942).

Brooks, Van Wyck, *The Ordeal of Mark Twain* (1920, 1933).

Canby, H. S., *Turn West, Turn East* (1951).

Carter, Paul, "The Influence of W. D. Howells upon Mark Twain's Social Satire," University of Colorado *Studies* (1953).

Cox, J. M., "*A Connecticut Yankee in King Arthur's Court*: The Machinery of Self-Preservation," *Yale Review* (1960).

DeVoto, B., *Mark Twain's America* (1932).

Gibson, W. M., "Introduction" to *A Connecticut Yankee in King Arthur's Court* (1960).

Hill, Hamlin, "Introduction" to *A Connecticut Yankee in King Arthur's Court.*

Hoben, John B., "Mark Twain's *A Connecticut Yankee*: A Genetic Study," *American Literature* (1946).

Lorch, Fred W., "Hawaiian Feudalism and Mark Twain's *A Connecticut Yankee in King Arthur's Court*" American Literature (1958).

Moore, O. H., "Mark Twain and Don Quixote," *Publications of the Modern Language Association* (1922).

Neider, Charles, "Introduction" to *A Connecticut Yankee in King Arthur's Court* (1960).

Parrington, V. L., *Main Currents in American Thought* (1930).

Quinn, A. H., "Mark Twain and the Romance of Youth," *American Fiction* (1936).

Reiss, Edmund, "Afterword" to A *Connecticut Yankee in King Arthur's Court.*

Roades, Sister M. T., "Don Quixote and *A Connecticut Yankee," Mark Twain Quarterly* (1938).

Scott, A. L., "Mark Twain Looks at Europe," *South Atlantic Quarterly* (1953).

Sherman, Stuart P., "Mark Twain," *The Cambridge History of American Literature* (Volume 3), eds., W. P. Trent and others (1933).

Smith, Henry Nash, *Mark Twain's Fable of Progress: Political and Economic Ideas in "A Connecticut Yankee"* (1964).

Spiller, Robert E., and others, eds., *A Literary History of the United States* (1955).

Taylor, W. F., *The Economic Novel in America* (1942).

Wiggins, Robert A., *"A Connecticut Yankee* and *The Prince and The Pauper*: Structure and Meaning," *Mark Twain: Jackleg Novelist* (1964).

Wilson, R. H., "Malory in the *Connecticut Yankee,"* University of Texas *Studies in English* (1948).

Winterich, John T., "Foreword" to *A Connecticut Yankee in King Arthur's Court* (1942).

LIFE ON THE MISSISSIPPI ANALYZED

Questions to consider: Contrast the two parts of the book as to the philosophic point of view of Mark Twain. Why does Twain introduce characters who actually lived? What is the role played by the Mississippi River in this work? How does this work have an inspirational effect on the reader? How does Twain attack Sir Walter Scott?

Cairns, William B., *A History of American Literature* (1930).

Clemens, Samuel Langhorne, "Spring on the Mississippi," in *The American Year,* ed., H. H. Collins (1950).

DeVoto, B. A., "The River," *Mark Twain's America* (1951).

Ganzel, Dewey, "Twain, Travel Books, and *Life on the Mississippi, American Literature* (1962).

Gohdes, Clarence, "Mirth for the Million," *Literature of the American People* (1951).

Kriegel, Leonard, "Afterword" to *Life on the Mississippi* (1961).

Malone, D. H., "Analysis of Mark Twain's Novel *Life on the Mississippi,"* in *The Frontier in American History and Literature,* ed., Hans Galinsky (1960).

Rankin, J. W., "Introduction" to *Life on the Mississippi* (1923).

Schmidt, Paul, "River vs. Town: Mark Twain's *Old Times on the Mississippi," Nineteenth-Century Fiction* (1960).

Scott, A. L., "Mark Twain Revises *Old Times on the Mississippi," Journal of English and Germanic Philology* (1955).

Sherman, Stuart P., "Mark Twain," *The Cambridge History of American Literature* (Volume 3), eds., W. P. Trent and others (1933).

Ticknor, C., "Mark Twain's *Life on the Mississippi," Glimpses of Authors* (1922).

Wagenknecht, Edward C., "Introduction" to S. L. Clemens' *Life on the Mississippi* (1944).

THE MYSTERIOUS STRANGER ANALYZED

Questions to consider: What is the evidence in this work that indicates Twain's pessimism? Does the reader feel sorry for young Satan? Are the episodes contrived? Does the ending of the story seem satisfying to the reader? Why was the tale set in the distant past? Is Twain's own youth reflected in this story?

Bellamy, Gladys C., *Mark Twain as a Literary Artist* (1950).

Cowper, F. A. G., "The Hermit Story, as Used by Voltaire and Mark Twain," in *Papers . . . in Honor of . . . Charles Frederick Johnson,* eds., Odell Shepard and Arthur Adams (1928).

DeVoto, B., "The Symbols of Despair," *Mark Twain at Work* (1942).

Ferguson, DeLancey, *Mark Twain: Man and Legend* (1943).

Fussell, E. S., "The Structural Problem of *The Mysterious Stranger,*" *Studies in Philology* (1952).

Matthiessen, F. O., "Mark Twain at Work," *The Responsibilities of the Critic* (1952).

Parsons, C. O., "The Background of *The Mysterious Stranger,*" *American Literature* (1960).

_______, "The Devil and Samuel Clemens," *Virginia Quarterly Review* (1947).

Reiss, Edmund, "Afterword" to *"The Mysterious Stranger" and Other Stories* (1962).

Smith, H. N., "Mark Twain's Images of Hannibal," University of Texas, *Studies in English* (1958).

ANALYSIS OF MARK TWAIN AS A PERSON

Questions to consider: Are Twain's Hannibal, Missouri and Mississippi River experiences reflected in his writings? How did his living in the West and his travels in Europe affect his point of view? How did Twain's years of residence in Connecticut influence his writings? Does Twain's viewpoint shift from optimism to pessimism?

Allen, Jerry, *The Adventures of Mark Twain* (1954).

Blankenship, Russell, "Mark Twain," *American Literature (As an Expression of the National Mind)* (1931).

Bolton, Sarah K., *Famous American Authors* (1954).

Bridges, H. J., "Pessimism of Mark Twain," *As I Was Saying* (1923).

Brooks, Van Wyck, "Mark Twain in the East," *The Times of Melville and Whitman* (1947).

______, "Note on Mark Twain," *Chilmark Miscellany* (1948).

______, *The Confident Years: 1885-1915* (1952).

______, *The Ordeal of Mark Twain* (1920, 1933).

______, *The Times of Melville and Whitman* (1947).

Canby, H. S., "Homespun Philosophers," *Seven Years' Harvest* (1936).

Chesterton, G. K., "Mark Twain," in *Handful of Authors,* ed., G. K. Chesterton (1953).

Clemens, Samuel Langhorne, "Love Letters of Mark Twain," *Jubilee* (from *Atlantic Monthly*) (1957).

______, *Mark Twain's Notebook,* ed., Albert Bigelow Paine (1935).

______, *The Autobiography of Mark Twain,* ed., Charles Neider (1959).

Hagedorn, H., "Samuel Langhorne Clemens: 1835-1910," *Americans: A Book of Lives* (1946).

Herron, Ima Honaker, "Mark Twain and the Mississippi River Town," *The Small Town in American Literature* (1939).

Howells, W. D., "Boy of the Southwest," *Jubilee* (from *Atlantic Monthly*) (1957).

_______, "Mark Twain," in *"Criticism and Fiction" and Other Essays,* eds., Clara Marburg Kirk and Rudolf Kirk (1959)

_______, "My Mark Twain," in *Shock of Recognition,* ed., E. Wilson (1955).

Hubbell, J. B., "Mark Twain," *The South in American Literature, 1607-1900* (1954).

Mencken, H. L., "H. L. Mencken on Mark Twain," in *Bathtub Hoax,* ed., H. L. Mencken (1958).

Morris, W., "Available Past: Mark Twain," in *Territory Ahead* (1958).

Priestley, J. B., "The Novelists," *Literature and Western Man* (1960).

Schmittkind, H. T. and D. A. Schmittkind, "Samuel Langhorne Clemens," *Living Biographies of Famous Novelists* (1943).

Untermeyer, L., "Mark Twain," in *Makers of the Modern World,* ed., L. Untermeyer (1955).

Van Doren, M., "Century of Mark Twain," *Private Reader* (1942).

Wagenknecht, E. C., ed., "Little Girl's Mark Twain," *When I Was a Child* (1946).

Wecter, Dixon, *Sam Clemens of Hannibal* (1952).

LITERARY TECHNIQUES USED BY MARK TWAIN

Questions to consider: What was Mark Twain's aim in writing this work? Which are the most effective of the literary techniques he uses? Consider Twain's choice of words and his ability to write good dialogue. Note the unexpected twists of thought in Twain's similes. Is humor introduced for a specific purpose? How is "contrast" used for literary purposes? How does Mark Twain weave recollections of his own past into his material?

Bellamy, Gladys Carmen, *Mark Twain As a Literary Artist* (1950).

Blair, Walter, *Native American Humor* (1937).

Branch, E. M., *The Literary Apprenticeship of Mark Twain* (1950).

Brashear, Minnie M., and Robert M. Rodney, eds., *The Art, Humor, and Humanity of Mark Twain* (1959).

Buxbaum, Katherine, "Mark Twain and American Dialect," *American Speech* (1927).

Canby, H. S., *Turn West, Turn East* (1951).

Clemens, Samuel Langhorne, "Fenimore Cooper's Further Literary Offenses," in *Heritage of American Literature* (Volume 2), eds., L. N. Richardson, G. H. Orians, and H. R. Brown (1951).

———, "Fenimore Cooper's Literary Offenses," in *Shock of Recognition,* ed., E. Wilson (1955).

———, *"How to Tell a Story" and Other Essays* (1897).

Cummings, Sherwood, "Science and Mark Twain's Theory of Fiction," *Philological Quarterly* (1958).

DeVoto, B. A., "Critics of Mark Twain," *Mark Twain's America* (1951).

______, "Mark Twain and the Limits of Criticism," *Forays and Rebuttals* (1936).

______, "Mark Twain: The Ink of History," *Forays and Rebuttals* (1936).

Fatout, Paul, *Mark Twain in Virginia City* (1964).

Feinstein, George, "Mark Twain's Idea of Story Structure," *American Literature* (1946).

Fraiberg, Louis, "Van Wyck Brooks versus Mark Twain versus Samuel Clemens," *Psychoanalysis and American Literary Criticism* (1960).

Fried, M. B., ed., *Mark Twain on the Art of Writing* (1961).

Gerber, J. C., "Relation Between Point of View and Style in the Works of Mark Twain," *Style in Prose Fiction,* ed., H. C. Martin (1959).

Goold, Edgar H., Jr., "Mark Twain on the Writing of Fiction," *American Literature* (1954).

Hoben, J. B., "Mark Twain: On the Writer's Use of Language," *American Scholar* (1956).

Hoffman, Daniel G., *Form and Fable in American Fiction* (1961).

Krause, S. L., "Twain's Method and Theory of Composition," *Modern Philology* (1959).

Lang, Andrew, "The Art of Mark Twain," in *Mark Twain: Selected Criticism,* ed., Arthur L. Scott (1955).

Lynn, Kenneth, *Mark Twain and Southwestern Humor* (1960).

Marx, L., "The Vernacular Tradition in American Literature," in *Studies in American Culture,* eds., J. J. Kwiat and M. C. Turpie (1960).

Matthews, Brander, "Mark Twain and the Art of Writing," *Essays on English* (1921).

Munson, Gorham B., "Prose for Humor and Satire," *Style and Form in American Prose* (1929).

Phelps, William Lyon, "The American Humorist: Mark Twain," *Some Makers of American Literature* (1923).

Rogers, F. R., *Mark Twain's Burlesque Patterns: As Seen in the Novels and Narratives, 1855-1885* (1960).

Rourke, Constance, *American Humor: A Study of the National Character* (1931).

Smith, H. N., *Mark Twain: The Development of a Writer* (1962).

Wagenknecht E. C., *Mark Twain: The Man and His Work* (1935).

NOTES

NOTES

NOTES

NOTES